WINE

LORE,
LEGENDS
— AND —
TRADITIONS

WINE

LORE,
LEGENDS
— AND —
TRADITIONS

PAMELA VANDYKE PRICE

HAMLYN

Front jacket *Detail showing the sense of taste from The Five Senses by Philippe Mercier. The Bridgeman Art Library/Roy Miles Fine Paintings, London.*

Back jacket *The Pinot Noir grape photographed near Rully, Burgundy. Patrick Eager.*

Back jacket flap *Jerry Bauer.*

Endpapers *Demijohns or bombonas of wine in the installations of TORRES in the Penedès region of Spain. The Image Bank, London.*

Half title page *A 17th century engraved corkscrew, commemorating a cock fight. Christie's Wine Department.*

Title page *The Mary Evans Picture Library.*

Published 1985 by Hamlyn Publishing
a division of The Hamlyn Publishing Group Ltd
Bridge House, 69 London Road
Twickenham, Middlesex

Copyright © Pamela Vandyke Price 1985

ISBN 0 600 32521 0

Set in 10/11½ Goudy
by Servis Filmsetting Ltd, Manchester
Printed in Italy

Contents

Preface   7

Some traditions   11

Old wives' witterings   31

Wine appurtenances   41

Varieties of *vin*   77

Well – what *is* in the name?   83

Champagne and its niceties   105

The wine game   119

Drink and diplomacy   129

. . . and women   139

. . . and pong   163

The last glass   169

Index   174

Acknowledgments

It is quite impossible to cite the names of all those who have contributed to this book because, as the reader will appreciate, it is in many instances a compilation of conversations, letters and reminiscences of friends, past and present, from all over the world of wine. Colleagues and other writers have generously encouraged me to quote from their own books and articles and, as on previous occasions, I am extremely grateful for the kindness of many associations in the wine trade, the information services of the main wine producing countries, librarians to whom I have referred queries of a special nature, including the librarian at Goldsmiths' Hall and, once again, The Guildhall Library.

Then I should like to thank the publishers, Hamlyn, whose enthusiasm and encouragement enabled me to complete the text quickly and, particularly, Stella Vayne, whose work in editing the book has been both tactful and intelligent, thereby improving it considerably.

Most of all I must thank my dear agent, Carole Blake. This is the first book I have written since she has been looking after my writing and the support and belief in me that she and, indeed, all her colleagues have shown throughout, has made an enormous difference to a work that will, I hope, justify their confidence and reciprocated affection.

Pamela Vandyke Price, 1985

Pamela Vandyke Price has also written:

The Art of the Table
Cooking with Wine, Spirits, Beer and Cider
Casserole Cookery
Cooking with Spices
France: a food and wine guide
The Wine Lover's Handbook
Wines and Spirits
Eating & Drinking in France Today
Directory of Wines & Spirits
Entertaining with Wine
The Taste of Wine
Guide to the Wines of Bordeaux
Guide to the Wines of Champagne
Dictionary of Wines and Spirits
The Penguin Book of Spirits and Liqueurs
Understanding Wines and Spirits
Enjoying Wine – a taster's companion
The Century Companion to the Wines of Bordeaux
The Penguin Wine Book
The Century Companion to Champagne
Alsace Wines & Spirits

Preface

This book is made up of information, often anecdotal, about wine. It might, in former times, have been described as 'table talk'. As novels and contemporary accounts indicate, people of past centuries did 'discuss' drink, in the sense of the word that means 'investigate', or 'try'. They do not, however, seem to have been particularly obsessed with food, in the way which prompts so many to discuss 'cuisine' today.

This may have been because, leaving aside very special occasions and large-scale feasts, the British, when they were fortunate enough to have had adequate amounts to eat, ate pretty well. In the first Elizabethan age, visitors from other countries remarked on the plenty and the quality of the basic ingredients. The fairly small population of England (until the curious and so far unexplained population explosion in the early part of the 19th century, before the real industrial age brought millions into towns and cities) meant that, to those in authority, life was not as cheap as it might be in more thickly populated countries. If you were of the nobility, you had to feed your fighting men, if you were of the merchant or middle class you had to feed your servants and clerks. Of course there were plagues and all classes might suffer from various diet deficiencies. But Queen Elizabeth I's black teeth, due to her eating too many sweets, were virtually a status symbol, and though the bad breath produced by bad digestion is frequently commented on in English literature, the British Isles did not, until comparatively recently, suffer from the appalling nutritional deficiencies that affected national health elsewhere. Nor do we appear to have endured the terrible famines that devastated parts of Europe from time to time, until the 19th century and the dreadful failure of the potato crop in Ireland.

Something taken for granted is rarely the subject of much talk or discussion. Those fortunate enough to live in countries where the climate is fairly reliable do not waste words on exchanging remarks about the weather! So the table talk of our ancestors seems to have stressed the aspects of the drink they had before them rather than the fare. Certainly all kinds of alcoholic drinks, imported or locally produced, were available.

Today, however, table talk may rather include the exchanging of recipes, or comment on what one has eaten in which restaurant; it may discuss the availability of many previously unknown and exotic foods, due to the influx of peoples from overseas. There's currently something of a reaction against wine talk, as being either snobbish, show-offish, or plain boring. The fact that we British can buy the wines of the world, in all price ranges, in a greater variety of retail outlets than any other country in the world, may tend to make us a little less appreciative of wine than we should be; the wine snobs have deterred many from even a meek attempt to understand the wonder that is wine and have inhibited the enjoyment that is so easy to achieve.

So if I called this book a compilation of 'wine talk' many people would not look into it, supposing it to contain detailed reports on vintages, accounts of world-famous tastings, solemn pronouncements about the qualities of certain wines and anecdotes about some of the great wine personalities, thereby indicating the writer's familiarity with all of them. Books like this do exist, but, although I may find them of some interest – sometimes they have an irritant value that may produce the pearl from my own work – I don't think they are intended to appeal to many of those people who would thoroughly enjoy sitting round a table, listening to conversation such as I have enjoyed as a guest of the hospitable wine trade during the last thirty years.

There are many quite odd bits of information that I have gleaned in this way, others that I have come upon in books, not necessarily wine books, or in hearing the family reminiscences of members of the wine trade, which they have simply never bothered to write down. If I must put a name to this book implying that it is about the 'curiosities' of wine, it's possible, in these permissive days, that some might search – in vain – for snigger-provoking anecdotes. So I prefer to think of this as a selection of what may unpretentiously be called 'carafe conversation', snippets of tales about wine, its use and conventions, such as a group of friends might exchange around a table graced with good food and, certainly, good wine, in relaxed circumstances.

There is one great omission from this book. Almost since records have been kept, wine has been associated with religion and religious rituals. Not only is this a subject virtually requiring a book to itself, but the number of Christian saints associated with the evolution and history of wine – leaving spirits out of the subject – is enormous and would certainly have made this book of unwieldy proportions.

Otherwise, of course, there are sure to be omissions. A reader may exclaim in annoyance that I have not included some particular stories that he or she has known for many years and found fascinating – but one cannot know everything. Nor is it possible to set down all that one does know at one time. If this account of some of the things that have interested me provokes a response about matters that have interested readers, I shall be delighted to hear from them.

Another omission is that of the work of other writers about wine. Possibly, as I might wish to comment on these, this is as well! But what others have written is, for the most part, widely available, although the contribution of some of the wine writers of the past has never yet been assessed in detail. Nor have I included the numerous (and often tired) quotations about wine that come out almost annually in anthologies for Christmas. Past poets and many otherwise distinguished novelists sometimes have very odd and uninformed things to say about wines, although there is much that indicates knowledge – and is still current – in the writings of Trollope, Peacock, Meredith, Surtees and their contemporaries. But as I can't find Dickens enjoyable and deplore the neglect of what I might term 'gutsiness' in the works of Jane Austen and the Brontës and as some of the great Victorian novelists were abstainers from drink, I've left them all out.

With love to
Margaret Howard
cherished guest
acclaimed hostess
whose perspicacity about wine is a
delight to all who know her

Some traditions

Certain traditions associated with wine are very old indeed. A cup of wine shared between friends or members of the same community has had special significance ever since records have been kept: whether the shared cup has been purely social or part of a religious ritual does not matter – when it is offered, it has special meaning and importance and, therefore, the gestures of offering and acceptance are usually formal. Sharing food and drink is one of the oldest rituals in the world. Whether a guest is offered a drink by the host or a special beverage in a special cup initiates an occasion, the moment is of significance.

The Anglo-Saxon equivalent of 'Cheers' was 'Waes hael!' signifying 'Be of good health!'. From this derives the wassail bowl or cup and its contents, which, even now, usually includes some of the spices and fruits that might have been used in its preparation many centuries ago. In primitive and early medieval times, the wife of the host or daughter of the house would offer the cup of welcome to any guest, bearing into the hall what was often a large and frequently a covered vessel, from which she would then take the first sip, indicating that the drink was wholesome. Some of the surviving ceremonial vessels have glass at the bottom, so that, as the drinker raised the bowl, using both hands, he could at least see if anyone was adopting a threatening attitude nearby. The cover of such a ceremonial cup might have been used to keep the contents warm, although my own theory is that it was a hygienic measure, to prevent the drink from being contaminated by any bird or bat droppings from the rafters of the ancestral hall or farmhouse, or, maybe, to prevent some exuberant bystander from dipping a finger in to sample the drink. The graceful drinking vessels of ancient Greece and Rome often had two handles, so that they could be passed from one drinker to another, frequently while reclining around the dining-table, as was customary. (Though eating propped sideways on a couch could not have been conducive to good digestion.)

Although wishing someone good health by means of raising a glass or sharing a drink from the same cup is a very old custom, the actual word, 'toast' comes into the language quite late – in the latter half of the 17th century, according to the Shorter Oxford Dictionary.

It appears that a morsel of toast was

often placed on the surface of the goblet of wine, perhaps sprinkled with spices or other flavourings, and that this was in some way associated with the name of a particular individual. I cannot discover much about this odd procedure, although it may be a curious ancestor of the dip or dunk. Perhaps if an inferior wine were being used, the toast was actually the best bit of the drink. My imagination toys with Poohsticks, alphabet soup, the more contorted and frivolous forms of pasta, but perhaps drinkers of that period had the toast thrown into the drink much as we would offer a side dish of crisps or nuts. Or could they, like the players of 'Kottobos' in ancient Greece (see page 21) have played some sort of game with a big bowl of punch or similar mixed drink, each drinker flinging in a bit of toast, accompanied by crying of an individual name and waiting to see whether each named bit sank or swam?

Two-handled drinking vessel – a kylix – which would have been used at a symposium, a drinking party for conversation and exchange of views on an intellectual plane, while the diners reclined. The kylix is often decorated with mythological drinking scenes, featuring women as well as men. (It is shown here from above.)

left The Swan Mazer, late 14th century (the foot was added in the 16th century). This was given to Corpus Christi College, Cambridge, by John Northwode, who entered the College sometime before 1384. It is a 'joke' drinking vessel, because, if the bowl is filled above the level of the central battlements, the liquid is siphoned out through a tube – giving the impression that the swan is drinking it. The mazer – mazers were often associated with the drinking of mead – originally had a cover.

The theory was that, in some way, the piece of toast was the prime morsel of the drink. So, when one fashionable man about town managed to obtain and quaff a goblet of the water in which the lady he admired had been bathing, a witty friend, (one of those characters who initiate something really important but whose name we shall never know), commented that he didn't mind not tasting the bathing beauty's bathwater, as long as he might 'have the toast' – that is, the lady herself. Whether toast as an ingredient in drink continued to be used, I don't know, but the expression caught on in smart talk and the word became a verb.

At the same time, the word 'bumper' came into the language implying – again according to the Shorter Oxford Dictionary – a drinking vessel filled to the brim. The wine lover of today, who is probably accustomed to enjoying wine in a glass of moderate or generous size, which will certainly not be filled to the brim if the pourer knows anything about the correct service of wine, may be astonished at the accounts of brimming bumpers being tossed off by our ancestors. But of course, as a visit to a museum will confirm, the glasses of past times were often very much smaller than ours, so that even a full glass would not have contained more than a gulp.

B.C. 668–627, King Ashurbanipal enjoys a drink with his queen in the royal garden, under an arbour of vines (the grapes seem to have been encouraged to grow upwards). Note that both are being fanned and that the lady has another smaller goblet in her left hand, so that, maybe, additional flavourings could be added to taste – some vessels intended for these are on the table.

14

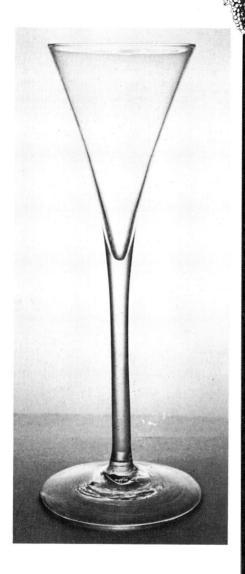

A toasting glass, from about 1760 – with a 'trumpet' bowl, holding a small amount of wine and a stem easily snapped between the fingers, so that the glass could never be used for a less worthy toast.

right Bacchus, depicted as a plump, vaguely oriental type by Caravaggio (1573–1610), extending a tazza, a wine cup with a shallow bowl and circular foot, an obvious descendant of the kylix.

The size of many toasting glasses makes this obvious. It is curious that, whereas 'to toast' signifies the salutation made in drinking the health of the person named, there is no verb now 'to health'. 'To wassail', or serenade even fruit trees, so that they may bear 'full many a plum and many a pear' is an outdated verb now as well.

Healths have often been drunk with the command 'No heel taps!' coming from the host or commander of the feast. This means that the glass should be drained, down to the dregs. The curious expression derives from the wedge of leather that used to be added to a shoe so as to increase the height of the heel; in the 18th century it began to be applied to the draining of wine at the bottom of any glass – in the days before much was known about filtration (and indeed when it may not have been practised at all) these dregs might have looked like a slither of leather, if one thinks of this as being akin to the 'lift' that today may be inserted under the heel inside a shoe. 'Heel tap' glasses are those that have no foot, so that, once filled, they must be emptied before they can be put down, upside down, like a stirrup cup (see page 19).

Those who raise their glasses to say 'Skaal!' or 'Skoal!', according to the Scandinavian language they are speaking, may not realise that the word derives from the old Norse 'Skalle' or 'Skull', and commemorates the high and far-off times when warriors were accustomed to drink from the skulls of their enemies. There are many complex conventions associated with this toast,

according to the country in which you are: the person who is 'Skaaled' or to whom you raise your glass, may have to stand, look into your eyes and perhaps link arms with you while you drink; it can be very discourteous to 'Skaal' the hostess, as she will certainly have to remain sober and therefore cannot return a number of toasts.

It is usually said, by the drinkers of schnapps, that the first schnapps must be downed in one – 'No heel taps' again – but that you can 'bite' the second in two and the third in three. In other words, you can take two sips at the second glass and three at the third. Another old custom was that a schnapps should be drunk for every button on the white waistcoat once traditional with evening dress; the man who sported a number of buttons was therefore also vaunting his capacity to drink.

I f someone raises his or her glass in the direction of an individual, or announces that he or she wishes to 'take wine' with a particular section of the assembled company, as still occurs at many dinners, it is obviously extremely rude to refuse to drink, although the person or persons honoured drink after the glasses have been raised to them. In former times – and not so long ago either – it would have been an insult to refuse to acknowledge the salutation and to drink subsequently; refusal to honour a toast was often for political reasons. When diners clink glasses across the table or with a neighbour, they are doing something that has associations with a particularly attractive legend. According to this tale, in the beginning of the world all the senses came before Dionysus, the God of Wine, to express their thanks for the joy that the blood of the grape had

A coaching glass, similar to a stirrup cup. The facet-cut knop or knob at the end of the stem makes the glass impossible to put down until it is emptied and can be upturned. This dates from about 1820, but the thrifty often filed off damaged feet on glasses so that they could be used in this way henceforth.

above left The Bayeux Tapestry, showing the Normans feasting, with Bishop Odo saying grace at the high table – right – William the Conqueror on his right. The meal is announced by the blast on a horn – possibly to be utilised for drinking later? The fare includes spit-roasted chickens, bread – of which the elderly diner is partaking immediately – and the butler, shown with napkin over left arm, is bringing a crock of wine to the diners.

below left An early version of the 'Elgin' glass? In fact, a pair of decorated Karchesia drinking goblets, which would have held more, for the Romans of classical times, than the shallow kylix.

brought to them. The eyes (the sense of sight), the hands (the sense of touch), the nose (the sense of smell), the tongue (the sense of taste) – all were delighted with their powers. Only the ear, the sense of hearing, remained dissatisfied and stood apart. Dionysus asked what the matter was?

'People can see wine, touch wine, smell wine, taste wine,' replied the ear, 'but no one *hears* wine.' 'Then,' said Dionysus, 'it shall henceforth be that, whenever men rejoice in each other's company and the wonder that is wine, they shall touch one cup against another, so that the chink, the chime, the delicate sound will preface their happy drinking – and its music shall please you.'

The word 'brimmer' is self explanatory. It is virtually the same thing as a bumper, a 17th century term, meaning a glass filled to the brim. A little, early 19th-century, quatrain records its use:

> My name is John Collins, head waiter at
> Limmer's,
> Corner of Conduit Street, Hanover
> Square.
> My chief occupation is filling the
> brimmers
> For all the young gentlemen frequenters
> there.

My friend John Doxat, who probably knows more about spirits, especially gin, than anyone else writing today, suggests that a 'brimmer' might at that time have been a type of 'sour', which is, or was, a spirit-based drink that also included fruit juice, sugar and mineral water. He thinks that the Tom Collins cocktail would have been this type of drink, made with the brand of gin called Old Tom, hence its name; other authorities on mixed drinks say that a John Collins uses only Hollands or Genever gin. I have no logical explanation for a feeling that, whereas the bumper appears to have been associated more with wine, brimmer could have been the term used when someone ordered a mixed drink. Yet it seems not beyond the bounds of possibility.

A custom that is definitely associated with brimming glasses, however, is the 'buzz'. 'To buzz' is a verb used when the bottle is sent round the table, people 'buzzing' the bottle, or pushing it onwards after helping themselves. This is certainly the sense in which the 19th century novelist Surtees uses it in his sporting novels. But, as a noun, buzz, which was originally spelt 'buz' appears in *Gryll Grange*, Thomas Love Peacock's novel, published in 1860.

Now another ploy is involved. As the decanter – buzzing seems mostly associated with port – arrives, a diner may suggest to the company that he has 'got a buzz', proving this by pouring all the wine remaining from the decanter into his glass, which the wine should then fill right to the brim, or even slightly bulge above. Wine writer Warner Allen (1881–1968), who had certainly observed buzzes, states that the possibility of a buzz would usually be the subject for a wager around the table: anyone who judged the remaining amount of wine correctly, filled his glass and thereby proved the point, would have another bottle paid for by everyone else. In our more moderate age, I believe

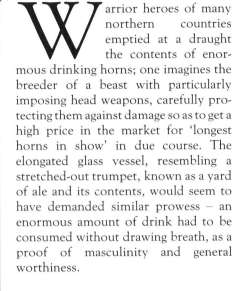

that anyone who achieves a buzz is merely given a helping from the fresh bottle that is thereupon ordered.

Throughout history, wine or some other alcoholic drink is made the subject of many games, wagers and proofs of skill or capacity. The ancient Greeks played a game of chance called 'Kottobos'; this seems never to have been described in exact detail and scholars present several theories about it, but it somehow involves swirling round the dregs in one's cup or glass, then flinging them out, so as to hit a determined mark on the floor or table.

Warrior heroes of many northern countries emptied at a draught the contents of enormous drinking horns; one imagines the breeder of a beast with particularly imposing head weapons, carefully protecting them against damage so as to get a high price in the market for 'longest horns in show' in due course. The elongated glass vessel, resembling a stretched-out trumpet, known as a yard of ale and its contents, would seem to have demanded similar prowess – an enormous amount of drink had to be consumed without drawing breath, as a proof of masculinity and general worthiness.

The idea of penalising by drink anyone who committed a gaffe or broke conventions in a way that offended the company, is also very old. Sometimes the offender is made to buy drinks for everyone at the table, sometimes he has

14th century drinking horn, mounted and trimmed with precious metal and decorations, plus feet to enable it to stand – a somewhat effete version of the enormous hollowed-out horns of primitive cattle, which Scandinavian warriors would have vied to drain without setting the horn down, or even taking breath. (The drinkers might well have collapsed afterwards.)

to drink off the contents of an intimidatingly large measure. In some of the older universities in Britain this latter penalty is known as sconcing, because of the use of a particular type of cup or mug called a sconce; some sconces are beautiful as well as historic works of art.

These days, however, our more sober society does not punish people by making them drink. Nor is the boast that someone is a 'four bottle man' or 'five bottle man' made any longer. It should be remembered that, in the days when hand-made bottles might vary considerably in their liquid contents, some wines could be drunk more quickly and easily than others. A contemporary equivalent I suppose might be the per capita pints of beer associated with certain sporting events, such as rugger and rowing, but the champions of today are more discreet about how much they can take.

English wine bottles: left to right, a green one, stamped 'Thomas Carlyon, 1708'; a round-ended pale brown bottle, 1630, which, because it couldn't have been stood upright, was probably used for pouring lavish helpings around the table, like the globular port decanter mentioned on page 28; the dumpy opaque glass bottle is somewhat larger than usual; the pale blue bottle, of about 1630, has a hollowed punt (the indentation underneath) and a ringed neck, to make it easier to grasp.

left *Detail of 'The Ham Luncheon' by Nicolas Lancret (1690–1743) indicates the accelerated consumption of drink as a result of the salty meat. Note the way in which the waiter, pouring into a smallish glass, is holding it by the foot, correctly. The 'patron' standing on the left suggests, by his expression, that there are too many breakages but the bottles vary in size. What looks like a cachepot on the table was probably a wine cooler.*

The ceremony of the Loving Cup is very old and picturesque. It must have taken place at many formal meals in the past, although nowadays it takes place mainly, if not solely, in the great halls of the City of London livery companies and the Mansion House, home of the Lord Mayor of London. (I am told that it is not always popular with those whose duties oblige them to attend a number of dinners including the ceremony, as it does prolong the occasion considerably, but it invariably delights visitors from abroad.)

The Loving Cup is prepared at the end of the meal and in fact several cups may be filled and in use at the same time. The procedure of serving and drinking is, however, always the same. The vessel used is a large one, somewhat like a deep chalice, with handles and, usually, a cover. The wine put into it is usually flavoured with some herbs and spices, just as it might have been centuries ago when wine kept a long time in wood might deteriorate to such an extent that only a few flavouring additives could make it palatable. The ceremony takes place at the end of the meal rather than the beginning, to indicate the fellowship and friendly feelings all now have for each other.

Three people are involved at a time and all stand up. The person on the right takes the cup, receiving it with a bow, turns to the man or woman on his or her left, bows, removes the lid from the cup if there is one and hands the cup to the person in the middle. This is the drinker, who bows when the cup is presented, then, using both hands to hold it, takes a drink, after which bows are again exchanged. The cover of the cup is then handed to the drinker, who puts it on the cup and turns to the left.

While this is going on, the person to the left of the drinker stands up and turns his back, so as to face the company. This is to guard the drinker who, with both hands occupied and attention directed to the drink, is vulnerable to any approaching enemy. People have indeed been stabbed in the back at such times. Such a crime would have always been regarded with particular horror, as desecrating a solemn moment when the drinker is supposedly at peace with the company around. Anyway, the guardian at the back ensures the drinker's safety.

The cup is then passed to the person on the left of the drinker, who receives it with a bow and another person stands to guard the back of the drinker while the procedure continues. The cup or cups circulate right round the table and there is generally some music played, often 'Drink to me only with thine eyes', while this is going on. When watching the company pledge one another and adopt the second person singular – 'Du' – way of address as a sign of friendship, in the party scene in Johann Strauss' opera *Die Fledermaus*, I have sometimes thought that an imaginative producer might make the singers indulge in a similar ceremony with their Champagne glasses, or maybe with one enormous glass. Though I suppose the routine followed might not be easy to time with the music – and drink on the stage is not, practically, usually alcoholic.

The wine which is most associated with a ceremony in its serving is port, particularly vintage port. Although the British still drink quantities of both the fine old tawnies and vintage ports, even in those countries that drink greater quantities of port than we do, the way in which the port is served has something specially British about it. It is not, usually, copied elsewhere, unless the host is lucky enough to have a British butler of the traditional type or has somehow trained local staff.

All the rituals associated with port are observed at the headquarters of the British Association in Oporto, known as the Factory House – the place where the British 'factors' or merchants, (now all of them port shippers) meet, lunch and give wonderful dinners and evening parties. There are the famous Wednesday luncheons at the Factory House for member shippers and their guests; these are restricted to men only. (The origin of the custom of ladies leaving the table at the end of a formal meal was to enable the men to get down to hard drinking, and, certainly in the 17th and 18th centuries – as is mentioned on page 134 – chamberpots were kept in the sideboards and servants were specially detailed to loosen the neck cloths of any gentlemen who rolled under the table and might risk choking from some form of fit. But although the visitor to the Factory House steps back in time, I have never heard of any similar scenes taking place there and, the wine trade being agreeably prone to gossip, I am sure the secret would have got out if they had.)

My friend Ben Howkins has described what happens at these Wednesday luncheons: 'Two ports are always served: an old tawny port, usually from the Treasurer's own firm, and a vintage port. Since 1856, it has been customary for all members, upon election, to present fourteen cases, equivalent to a quarter cask, of their firm's vintage port. . . . A game which never loses its fun or excitement is always played: guess the year and the shipper of the vintage port.' This game is also played on many occasions around the tables of the wine trade with fortunate guests. Sometimes participants are asked to guess the name and vintage of a table wine earlier in the meal; frequently, people will be asked to put some small sum of money into a pool, the person who guesses the wine correctly winning the total, although on many occasions the money is donated to the British wine trade's own Benevolent Association.

Ben Howkins' description of the Wednesday luncheon continues: 'The remarkable thing about the dining-room is that there are actually two rooms, both of identical size and each capable of seating forty-six persons. Two sets of folding doors lead from one room to the other. In the first room, where the Wednesday luncheons are held, members and their guests sit at a long mahogany table, with graceful chandeliers (now electrically powered) overhead. The second dining-room is where everyone moves to enjoy the vintage port; by tradition, just before this exodus takes place, you are served with a glass – only one – of delicious very old tawny port, always decanted, which is irreverently referred to as "mouthwash". The next moment everyone rises, napkins clutched in their hands, and all move through the doors to sit down in the adjoining room in exactly the same order as before, but here candles provide the only light, flickering on the lavish bowls of fruit and walnuts and reflected in the laden decanters. Now the vintage port can be enjoyed to the full without any aroma of food hanging in the air. Toasts are always proposed to "The Queen" and "The President of the Republic".' (From Rich, Rare and Red by Ben Howkins, Heinemann, 1982.) My own recurrent query is – why, when so much attention is paid to the clean atmosphere required for appreciation of the wine, do the diners retain their dirty – and possibly odoriferous – napkins? No one has ever been able to tell me. (Nor do I understand why, in photos and films of this hallowed place, there are scented flowers on the table and people light up after the toast.)

For the service of port in the ordinary way, the decanters would traditionally be put on the dining-table only after the cloth had been removed; table mats are a very recent innovation in Britain at formal meals, especially dinners. In a great household or smart mess, there would be no lifting and rolling of the cloth. Once any easily overturned or fragile objects had been removed, servants would literally jerk the cloth from under anything remaining on the table, having previously arranged it in a special way when they were laying-up. This is why some old damask table-cloths are very large in size; they didn't just cover the entire surface of the table, sometimes being doubled under. The port decanter – usually standing in a coaster, some of which are beautifully designed – was, and is, set in front of the host. The host then picks up the decanter and port drinking is about to begin.

The host is allowed a 'backhander', by which he fills the glass of whoever is on his right, otherwise he or she would have to wait for his or her port until the decanter had completed its circuit of the table. Some people achieve this backhander with a particularly graceful gesture, the back of the hand down, the decanter cradled on the forearm. The host then helps himself and passes the decanter to the left.

Sending the port the wrong way has been the subject of many cartoons and jokes and, in the days when people cared seriously about the conventions, was a shocking gaffe. Periodically, there is a query and a new set of theories in the trade and more serious press as to why the port goes round from right to left, clockwise, rather than the other way. Theories concerning the course of the earth around the sun, the bad luck and black magic associated with going widdershins (anti-clockwise), the very primitive belief in the right hand being for important and good actions, the left for less worthy ones (as in certain tribal rituals of hygiene, only the right hand is used for eating), have all been advanced and I can even remember some association with Stonehenge being brought into a discussion of this kind. But in fact, except for anyone left handed, it is much easier to pass the port from one's own place over to the left. Experiment and see – if you

Dining-room in the Factory House in Oporto, showing the table set for forty-six gentlemen, with showcases in the background displaying the superb sets of antique china.

push the decanter to your right, it may knock into your own glasses and whoever is on your right hand will have to stretch over to take hold of it: whereas, if it goes to the left, it should have no obstacles in its way before arriving at the glass of your neighbour. The long necks of most decanters, for table wines as well as port, facilitate passing them and the ridges that are often seen on the necks of traditional port decanters provide a good grip if the decanter has to be lifted.

At times when table gimmicks were very popular, various intricately worked miniature carts or carriages, with wheels, would serve for pushing the decanter or decanters – sometimes Madeira or even old claret would be an alternative to port – around the table; Ben Howkins tells of the delightful 'railway' that moves them across the fireplace in the Senior Common Room in New College, Oxford. This was made

about 1820, after a guest, trying to pass the port across the fireplace, slipped and fell, with the decanter in his hand. I am quite sure that the main concern of the company on that occasion was the waste of the wine rather than any injury to the guest. For brisk circulation, some people serve port from a decanter with a globular base, which cannot be set down at all; it sits in a frame which is set in front of the host. He then passes the decanter on but keeps the frame in its original place, so that no one can put the decanter down until it has been around the table. This seems somewhat awkward, but it has its origin in another example of good manners.

It is a breach of courtesy to ask for the port decanter to be passed to you – your neighbour is obliged to keep an eye open for anything you require. So a polite phrase is sometimes used to indicate the wish of one diner to have the bottle or decanter passed after too long a wait at one place. 'Do you know Dr. Wright of Norwich?' or 'The Bishop of Norwich', or a reference to some possibly invented character may then be heard. In fact there really was a Dr. Wright of Norwich, who, in the middle of the 19th century, gained a great reputation both for being extremely sociable and also a 'bottle stopper', so that people would ask for the port by using his name, indicating that the decanter should be moved along. The apparent irrelevance of such a query and a meaningful look from the thirsty inquirer, usually jolt the offender into realising that he has stopped the bottle. Apparently the original Dr. Wright took the query in good part when it was directed at him.

left *One of a pair of silver gilt coaster 'wagons', made in 1828 by Benjamin Smith, for the first Earl of Hastings, bearing his arms. The articulated coaster would be wheeled around the dining-table, possibly bearing two different wines. Note the loops – versions of vine branches, in which the decanter stoppers could be rested.*

In the 1870s nearly all the vines of western Europe were destroyed by Phylloxera. Most European vines are now grafted onto Phylloxera-resistant American stocks. During the 7–10 years before the new vines were bearing fruit, the English port shippers in Oporto subsidised the Portuguese farmers. One farmer directed in his will that when the descendants of Cockburn Smithes came up the Douro river each year to inspect the crop, there should, in perpetuity, be a man waiting for them with a live turkey and a sack of almonds. The picture shows John Smithes receiving the gift.

It was always impressed upon me, when, about thirty years ago, I began to attend luncheons and dinners at which port was served, that it was also rude to pass the decanter without helping oneself, even to the putting of a mere few drops into one's glass as a gesture. I suppose the origin of this dates from a long way back, when refusal to share a drink implied that you suspected poison. This convention seems seldom in use today.

These days, when lengthy sessions of heavy drinking are unlikely to take place after the meal, it is not unusual for the port to circulate before the company leaves the table all together, or else the ladies are provided with a decanter in the drawing-room. Perhaps, as this is likely to be a cleaner, fresher atmosphere, they get the best of the deal this way, like those who progress from one dining-room to another at the Factory House!

Old wives' witterings

A number of curious beliefs surround wine, which often deter the would-be drinker by conveying the impression that wine is difficult to enjoy.

One oft-quoted maxim is to the effect that one should not mix 'grape with grain', in other words, drink both spirits and wine in a short space of time. The belief seems to be that you risk more of a hangover or get drunk faster if you do this. But it is the word 'mix' that is operative, for, if you consume a number of different drinks, without much discrimination, you are liable to get an upset stomach and an upset stomach is at least part of the horrors of the classic hangover. It is also sense, if you are planning to drink fine and delicate wines, not to stun the palate beforehand by something extremely high in alcohol and, maybe, assertive in its taste.

If you have had a dry martini, or a couple of double gins and tonic, or a generous measure of Scotch, or a large Bloody Mary, then you are unlikely to be able to appreciate the fragrance and delicate flavours of, say, a fine Mosel immediately afterwards. This is not to say that any of the spirit drinks are bad – only that they can overwhelm such a subsequent wine, though there are plenty of robust wines that may hold their own on the palates of even fairly heavy spirit drinkers. Some people assert that brandy, the spirit of wine, will not produce harmful effects if mixed in in this way, but, obviously, this rather depends on the amount and, certainly, the quality of the brandy! If you tip into your stomach in fairly rapid succession a variety of spirits, wine and other beverages, such as might compose the more complicated type of Regency punch, then you should not be surprised if, later on, you have the sort of reaction often described by Regency rakes. One shudders at the prospect of dealing with oneself at a time when aspirin, health salts, and similar medicaments had not yet been invented, although, as Lord Byron said, 'Let us have wine and women, mirth and laughter, Sermons and soda water the day after.' (*Don Juan*, II, clxxviii.)

There is a similar belief that port and Champagne should never be combined at the same meal, though I've never met anyone suffering ill-effects as a result of the combination and I have certainly enjoyed meals that began with Champagne and ended with port.

Then there is the belief that something terrible will occur if anyone eating oysters drinks whisky at the same time, though several oyster bar owners have assured me that they have known customers who regularly consume this combination without any apparent ill-effects at all.

Related to this again is the 'white wine with white meat, red wine with red' dictum, which some British still believe and which is still cited in many of the 'Instant Winemanship' manuals. I have never been able to make anyone explain to me, however, why roast chicken or turkey with all the trimmings of stuffing, sausages, dark gravy, are 'white' and why a dish such as

A voluptuary, under the horrors of digestion. Gillray's portrayal of George IV – note the medicinal potions, including 'Vegetable syrup', on the side, and the numerous bills underneath the chamberpot.

blanquette de veau is 'red'. And where do you put roast pigeon or rabbit? This is all rather like the alternating 'red and white' diet of Davey Warbeck, in Nancy Mitford's *The Pursuit of Love*, when he has an egg instead of saddle of mutton as his 'white' meal, saying how next morning's breakfast kippers were for his 'red' meal – ' "Brown counts as red". . . . But when a chocolate cream . . . came round, it was seen to count as white.'

Anyone clinging to such notions risks being severely shocked if voyaging in any of the wine countries, where, especially if red, white and pink wines are all made in the same region, the locals happily drink whatever they like whenever they feel like doing so. Some people do get a slightly metallic taste in their mouth if they drink red wine with white fish, but there are plenty of us who will cheerfully drink a red wine with, say, grilled sole, poached turbot – and the classic Loire dish, Saumon Chambord, is actually cooked in the region's red wine! Traditionalists must have a terrible time when faced with some of the delicious Spanish and Mediterranean dishes that combine meat and fish in the same recipe.

One of the most fascinating tastings I ever arranged was to discover the wine or spirit that most agreeably accompanied that problem food – smoked salmon. The wine trade contributed numerous suggestions, including schnapps, old Sauternes, malt whisky, and even a small-scale regional claret. Although, attempting to taste the various drinks while I still had the taste of the smoked salmon in my mouth, I repeatedly spat the salmon down the spittoon and swallowed the drink, I did emerge with the feeling that perhaps the most satisfactory accompaniment was the Portuguese white vinho verde, with its slight sparkle and fairly tough, dry character. But this is a subject that can provoke endless discussion around a dinner table, so there can be no question of absolute right and wrong.

Indeed, rigid advice about 'what to drink with what' can be misleading: for example, look up what a number of respected authors have said about the wine that should accompany ham; few of them take into account the way the ham has been cooked, what it was like as ham originally, type of cure, where it has come from, which sort of beast (male or female, of what age) has provided it; whether there is a sauce, what it was cooked with – fruit? Mustard? Spices? What the accompaniments are by way of vegetables. Tomatoes or garlic can take over a dish, carrots can sweeten it and so on. And, of prime importance, are the questions as to what wine went before the ham course and what is likely to come after? To generalise about a single course in the middle of a meal that may include several strongly-flavoured dishes and other drinks is just silly. Indeed, if I'm reviewing a book about wine and haven't time to go right through it, the 'what to drink with what' section often determines whether I pay any serious attention to the writing or throw the book aside as being comparatively

A wedding party enjoying whatever the wine of their region happens to be, white or, as in this instance, red, in dumpy tumblers.

worthless. Alas, some eminent wine writers have been misguided enough to generalise on the subject, often not even specifying anything more than the wine's name; indeed, one very famous authority simply said 'Montrachet' was to be served with ham. He specified neither the wine's vintage nor origin – both of which facts could have made a considerable difference. Was it a grower's wine or one from the big négociants? But, in his day, it didn't matter so much, we didn't think we knew so much – but the facile advice continues; it's inadequate, encourages few and may deter many.

In the last few years, a more interesting condition than the conventional hangover has been scientifically established, which Professor Goldberg, of the University Hospital of South Manchester, names 'redhead'. Sufferers develop a severe headache and nausea some time after they first wake up on the morning after drinking even a small amount of red wine. The appalling thing is that sufferers can't lie down, because the headache then intensifies. But if they stand up the nausea gets worse. There are a number of conflicting theories as to the exact cause of 'redhead'. Some people find that, with very old red wines of fine quality, they do not suffer any ill effects, but of course one can hardly drink costly and choice bottles every day. The way the wine is made and any treatment to which it is subjected also appear to be factors influencing this condition. But because some

Pickers in the Muscadet country. By the end of the vintage, there will be some just-made wine to sample – but it will be cloudy and, although delicious, should only be taken in small quantities.

people reasonably enough shy away from any red wine, the considerate host will always have something white available as well.

There are some curious proverbs associated with drink and wine, including one to the effect that you should 'Drink as much after an egg as after an ox', and another to the effect that, 'If you drink in your pottage (porridge) you'll cough in your grave'. This may refer to the belief still held by some people that one should not drink anything liquid during a meal; my own grandfather apparently refused to allow water on the table in his household, (he couldn't have afforded wine) saying, 'You don't put your food on top of a lake'.

On the other hand, another saying is 'Do not drink between meals' (1609); 'Garlic makes a man drink' and the cynical, 'Drink wine and have the gout; drink no wine have the gout too', are others. The latter in fact is sound, because it is now known that gout is not related to excessive consumption of alcohol at all.

Then there's an odd saying, 'Milk says to wine welcome'; but this certainly refers to the usually pleasing combination of the acidity in the wine and the alkalinity in the milk or milk product, which is why wine (not necessarily red wine), is such a good partner to cheese.

One of the most prevalent misconceptions about wine, however, is to do with salads. A proverb says that one 'Drinks not wine after salad' and another that one should 'Take heed of vinegar of sweet wine'. I don't know about the vinegar of sweet wine, as it is the acidity that makes good vinegar (I speak as one who makes her own), and sweet wine vinegar sounds a treacherous concoction, at best a contradiction in terms.

The clash of wine with salad is more complex. It is the vinegar bacillus (acetobacter) that 'turns' wine, which is why, in many wine regions, notably Jerez, where sherry vinegar, which may be as old as a hundred years, is prized almost more than the wine, it is obligatory to keep the vinegar casks in a separate building. Even a small quantity of spilt wine that is not cleaned up within a winery may have an adverse effect on the wine around it, which is why scrupulous cleanliness is essential in wine making. Any drops of wine left over in an uncorked bottle from someone's lunch can do real harm if forgotten and remaining within the vicinity of young wines. But it should be remembered that this refers to wine vinegar – not malt vinegar, which is referred to as 'beeregar and alegar' in the early documents of the Worshipful Company of Distillers in the City of London.

The British, traditionally fond of 'beef and beer', have also always been particularly fond of vinegar, which must be usually assumed to be malt vinegar. The late Raymond Postgate said that this was only useful for stripping varnish from furniture. I would not go quite as far as this, because malt vinegar can be acceptable when sprinkled on fish and chips in newspaper and appropriate circumstances. However, it is undeniable that malt vinegar is far more assertive and indeed aggressive in flavour than wine vinegar – and it is this flavour to which the British palate is accustomed. (Many fish and chip shops do not, as my friend Derek Cooper has discovered, serve real vinegar at all – only something supposedly resembling it in flavour.)

Recipes for pickles and chutneys seldom specify wine vinegar. Mine, made with my own wine vinegar, are much milder than any commercial products I have ever tried and they may indeed be more in the nature of rather savoury conserves: of course, this does not do away with the fact that they contain vinegar and, logically, if this meets with wine in the mouth, it 'turns' the wine – in other words, the vinegar takes over and makes the wine into vinegar.

There are several reasons, however, why the enjoyment of salad need not conflict with the enjoyment of wine: first, at conventional and formal British meals salad is not served at all and, in the traditions of 'cuisine', as observed in France and other countries, when salad is served, it comes after the main dish of the meal, when the accompanying wine might be expected to have been finished. (The British, incidentally, are also extraordinary in that they serve a sweet course before cheese, although after anything sweet the appreciation of, say, a fine red wine is virtually impossible. And as for those who would then accompany what remains in the decanters by a savoury, that particular British speciality, most savouries – angels on horseback (oysters encased in bacon), anchovies on toast, or the spicy tit-bits with which the habitués of the coffee and gaming houses of former times refreshed themselves, perking up their palates to be better able, later on, to tackle any serious consumption of port – are absolutely inimicable to wine. Perhaps the definition of 'salad' should be more clearly thought out! The British serve it – or don't serve it – in one way, other nations in other ways.)

The main objection to serving salad, in these more relaxed times, in the course of a meal that may include good wine, is not, in my view, to the salad itself. It relates to the composition of the salad dressing. I am taking it for granted that, in this context, the term 'dressing' does not apply to mayonnaise or any of the creamy, eggy dressings that can be very good, but which, used with a salad intended to set off a main course and refresh the diner, merely pile richness on richness and make appreciation of the wine very difficult. But the tradition-al 'French dressing' or 'vinaigrette', as many Britons make it and as many cookery books describe it, is about as fierce an antagonist for any fine wine that could be imagined.

The proportions for this 'dressing' tend to be three of oil to one of vinegar, though I have come across recipes that specify half and half, or two to one. The whole thing is mixed up together in advance, including salt, pepper, mus-tard and anything else thought likely to enhance the mixture – which it does not.

After much experimentation – and a comparative salad dressing tasting is a fascinat-ing thing to conduct – I am now quite firm that Alexandre Dumas'

advice, is sound. He got this from Comte J.A. Chaptal, (the minister whose signature to a decree permitting the addition of sugar to the 'must', gave the word 'chaptalisation' to the wine vocabulary). Chaptal apparently made a study of the subject and advocated adding the oil and, if liked, the mustard, to the salad bowl, then putting the salt and pepper on to the salad ingredients, because salt will not dissolve in oil; next turning the ingredients in the oil and, only at the last minute, adding the vinegar, because then the condiment can act in its true capacity. This, he affirms, is the right procedure. So say I. Of course, sometimes one has to mix all the ingredients together, but the idiocy of some waiters in preparing the dressing on a flat plate is obvious, for thereon it can't be properly mixed at all.

If you put the vinegar on at the last moment before serving, the salad will not wilt; the vinegar will spice the salad, as it should do, without its flavour dominating and it is this absence of dominance that, in my opinion, makes a salad so dressed perfectly acceptable after fine wine. At least, several eminent members of the wine trade have found it so at my own table.

It should perhaps be added that the proportions I allow for a salad are (slightly depending on the ingredients, some of which may be more absorbent than others), seven or even nine of oil to one of vinegar. That astounds people. It hasn't worried those who have eaten salads I have prepared.

I suppose we got into the habit of lavishing vinegar, from no matter what source, ale, beer, wine, on our meats and vegetables when it was at least some safety measure against the hazards of rotten food, but we don't need to assault our palates with it today. And in case people who think 'all that oil' is unacceptable, I would bring to their attention the fact that the bulk of the olive oil of Spain goes to the most famous maker of baby foods in the world – for unlubricated babies are unhappy babies. Oil, as such, need be in no way harmful although, if people do not wipe the neck of the receptacle from which the oil is poured, what is left on the outside may turn rancid and pollute subsequent pourings. It is this rancid flavour that people do not like and that, often without much reason, suppose upsets them.

I t should be appended to this note about salad, that, in one of the admirable thrillers by Robert Parker, whose private investigator is soundly gastronomic, I came across the recommendation to add a little honey to a salad dressing. On trying this, I found it excellent, honey being different in composition from sugar, so that, although I would not use sugar in a salad, except occasionally on tomatoes, the few drops of honey are now, to me, routine when I'm making a salad dressing.

F inally, there is the somewhat rollicking saying about the way a bottle is grasped: 'Hold a bottle by the waist, a woman by the neck' is the way in which I originally heard it, from someone who was certainly authoritative on women as well as wine. But there are those who say it should be 'Hold a bottle by the neck, a woman by the waist'. The latter version may show more consideration for the woman, but, if you pick up a bottle and pour, holding it by the neck, then there is not quite the same control over the flow as if it is held by the waist, nor can any deposit be seen as it comes up into the neck of the bottle. Although the latter half of the maxim may not appeal to 'liberated' ladies, even they will have to agree that the policy as regards the bottle is sound.

Wine appurtenances

There are a number of mysteries here. The sort of reader who writes letters beginning 'You are wrong about', or 'It is astonishing that you do not know', or even 'I have always been led to believe by . . .' (the authority cited being either obscure, or one with whom the writer has little sympathy), will have an enjoyable and active time, although I hope that much useful and odd information may be benevolently contributed to me as well. There are so many things one does not know, so little time – for the writer who does not enjoy the leisure conveyed by a private income – to research these fascinating matters and there is probably someone, somewhere, who has taken for granted something that puzzles me.

*The Burgundy bottle through the ages –
showing the different sizes and variations on
basic shapes.*

right *Various shapes and sizes of
Champagne bottles, showing the way the
agrafe, the metal clip, bites into the cork until
the period when the metal plaque on the top
of the second cork prevented this. One of the
bottles still has the cork tied down with twine,
prior to the evolution of the wire 'muzzle'. In
the background, the circular Champagne press
or maie.*

🍇 Bottles 🍇

It is easy to see, for example, how the 'Dame Jeanne' bottle became a demijohn, but where was it first made and what size was the original? The 'Marie Jeanne' of the Coteaux du Layon and Bordeaux contains one and one third litres, or one and three-quarters bottles and it looks like a magnum bottle – until you see the two side by side. One can understand the 'pot' of the Beaujolais, which contains half a litre, originating from a colloquial term for the bottle, but where did the dumpy clavelin, used for Jura wines, come from? Large bottles are increasingly popular today, when many inexpensive wines, suitable for parties, are sold in them. The large sizes are also used for the aristocrats of Champagne, Bordeaux and Burgundy. In case anyone wants to settle a bet, the following are the accepted Champagne bottles: a magnum is two bottles; a jeroboam is four, a rehoboam is six, a methuselah eight, a salmanazar twelve, a balthazar sixteen, a nebuchadnezzar twenty bottles. The Bordeaux jeroboam used to be six bottles, until 1978; it is now five litres, that is, 6.67 bottles in total, if one calculates the 'bottle' as containing approximately 75 centilitres. An impériale, which is sometimes used for fine claret, contains eight bottles and a big bottle called a Chiantigianna, used for Chianti, holds 1.75 litres.

The bulbous-shaped bottle used for some Chianti Ruffino, is known as a *magnifico*. It can be laid down on its side, unlike the rotund *fiasco*, and, therefore, is employed for wines that can be improved by maturation in bottle. The name seems to have originated in the United States, possibly the inspiration of a clever marketing person, maybe with Italian ancestry, and, as anybody

from Texas would certainly have us believe, anything 'magnificent' is better, bigger – and, sometimes, alas – more expensive. The big (2-litre size) wicker-covered flask used for the white wines of Orvieto is known as a *toscanello*, but I don't know that this has the same sort of sales appeal. The name is possibly confusing, because Orvieto is in Umbria, not Tuscany, as the word might suggest. The ordinary Orvieto wicker-bound flask is not identical with that of Tuscany's Chianti, because it contains about 75 centilitres whereas the Chianti fiasco holds a litre. But no one has ever been able to tell me why the names of Old Testament kings are used for the big Champagne bottles. Did some seminary-trained *caviste* (head cellarman) start using biblical nicknames for the big

bottles? Could the implications of age and antiquity relate to the way in which wine in large bottles tends to mature at a slower rate than that in ordinary bottles?

Two shapes of wine containers have rather curious origins, or, rather, origin, because both came from the wineskin. A whole skin, fastened at the top like a bag, served as a means of carrying wine, often slung on the saddle or attached to the packs of a beast of burden, for use on a journey in ancient times.

The most convenient size – for not everyone could afford, or indeed would have found it practical, to travel with a large quantity of wine at a time – was that

which, these days, is usually regarded as 'a bottle', or about 70–75 centilitres. In times before bottles were receptacles for wine that would be used for storage and long-term maturation, but were types of carafe, for bringing wine from the cask in the cellar to the table, too big a 'skin' would have been a risk; too small might seem mean and, in taverns and places where people bought drink, rather uneconomic. So the basic 'wineskin', as the medieval equivalent of the consumers' groups might have been said to have evolved it, was the skin of a goat's scrotum. (One shudders at the thought of what meagre measures might have resulted had other animals inhabited European wine regions.)

Sometimes people find it 'ughsome' to imagine wine being put into such a receptacle. They should be reminded that, while in most regions where grapes are crushed by the bare foot, the treaders wash their feet first, they sometimes don't bother to wear shorts, especially in remoter areas (and even in some of the vineyards of Burgundy). But anyone who really objects can be reassured that wine is the second oldest disinfectant in the world. The victim who 'fell among thieves' in the parable of the Good Samaritan, had his wounds washed with wine and dressed with oil. The acidity of the wine can be efficacious in the absence of TCP or any antibiotic. (And because somebody is certain to wonder what the oldest disinfectant in the world is, they can find out in T.E. Lawrence's *Seven Pillars of Wisdom*, in which the Arabs ask young boys to urinate on the wounds of those who survived a battle in the desert. The uric acid was at least some form of medicament – would you prefer to lose arm, leg, or life itself as a result of otherwise inevitable gangrene? A pity the remedy wasn't tried in the Crimea!)

The pisadores, *or treaders, preparing to start work in the sherry lagar, wearing their special* zapatos de pisar *boots. These have a special arrangement of nails on the sole, so that the pips and stalks are trapped, undamaged, without being split, which would make the wine harsh and bitter. Note the staves they carry – treading is hard, serious work, which takes place at night and in the cool of the morning so that the treaders can rest in the heat of the day. Now machines have largely taken over from this traditional process.*

left *'The Cellar Boy' by Jean-Baptiste Chardin (1690–1779), in which the young man carrying the cellar key is emptying out a pitcher, a vessel which might have served as a measure, after emptying the wine into the small vat. Note that his implement is wood – no metal is to be brought into contact with the wine – and that in the funnel in the bottle whisked eggwhites have been prepared with which to 'fine' the wine, attracting any particles in suspension within it.*

From the globular shape of the wineskin came the *boxbeutel*, the dumpy green bottle used for certain wines of Franconia, (more correctly those of the Steinberg vineyard), hence the generic name for them, 'Steinwein'. Skins were used in virtually every region to transport wine. In our own time, whole goatskins have been used to move the newly-made wine down from the less accessible vineyards and wineries of Madeira to where they could be loaded and taken down by lorries to the lodges in Funchal. Today, improved roads have made their use unnecessary.

From the wineskin as it was used in Spain came the *porrón*, the triangular-shaped flask, with a projecting spout, from which the drinker can pour wine into his mouth without the flask touching his lips. This had obvious advantages in times when hygiene was hardly understood. And, as those who have assisted in wine ceremonies in parts of Spain will know, the direction of the jet of wine is often subjected to detours by the skilled, running down the forehead and the nose before it gets to the mouth, or being tossed around on its way. The straw-encased flasks, traditional now for everyday quality Chianti and Orvieto, are also obvious derivations from the globular wineskin; the straw that partly covers the bulbous bottle prevents one bottle from banging against its neighbour with the risk of cracking the glass. As bottles would have been used again and again – unless actually broken – in times when glass was more expensive than it is today, the advantages of this form of protection are obvious, especially when vast quantities

Wine in whole goatskins being brought down from the mountain vineyards of Madeira by labourers in the pre-lorry era.

above right *Wine in biggish containers is still popular in taverns and among groups of workers for their daily ration. Here, the demijohns are awaiting collection outside the bodegas of Alvear, in Montilla, Spain.*

below right *Fitting the straw jackets around the fiaschi of certain Italian wines – now somewhat declining in use. Although some firms even use plastic for this, the dressing of the bottle in this way is now really outmoded with modern packaging, but it remains picturesque and appealing to the customer for wines of everyday quality, that do not require laying down for maturation.*

of *fiaschi* were loaded onto a cart, slung across a saddlepack, or festooned around the entrance to a wine shop.

A term that must have come into use fairly recently, but the origin of which I cannot trace, refers to a type of wine carafe or jug in which there is a pocket for ice on the side to keep the contents cool. This is known as a 'marsupial', from the generic name of the charming pouched creatures of Australia.

Owl-shaped cup, of a coconut mounted in parcel-gilt, 1556, from either Germany or Switzerland. The owl is associated traditionally with greed and drinking. The inscriptions on the cup are biblical and also say, 'When all birds are in their nests, my flight is the best of all.'

Glasses

There are glasses with names of specific wines attached to them. Patrick Forbes's book, *Champagne: the Wine, the Land, and the People* (Gollancz 1967) which is a work of art, as well as scholarship, shows on its cover a fairly shallow white porcelain cup, mounted on crystal, supported in a silver frame by rams heads. The rams have golden faces, fleeces and horns and their little golden hooves appear at the base of the frame. The porcelain cup is rather similar in proportion to a Chinese stem cup, the rim turning very slightly outwards, the base pointing down into a crystal holder in the centre of the frame.

This, the property of the Antique Company of New York Inc., is one of four *coupes* made in Sèvres porcelain, which were once in the Dairy Temple at the Château du Rambouillet, the property of Queen Marie Antoinette. It is said that these four coupes were moulded on the Queen's breasts. I do not know their date, but I would say quite definitely that, if this was so, then the moulds were taken when Her Majesty was lying down. (Or, maybe, the corsets of the epoch had made her a bit flat in the front.) The shape is a possible one for the enjoyment of sparkling wine, although the opacity of the porcelain masks colour and vivacity.

Most people know the shape of the *copita*, traditional for sherry, but few will probably be aware that its name is an affectionate diminutive for a whole *copa* and, therefore, means 'little cup' or small mouthful, somewhat similar to the Austrian 'Schluck' wine name, which means 'a gulp'. Glasses for wine have been made in a huge variety of shapes, including kneeboots – through association with the fetish of the shoe, I suppose – and these jokey drinking vessels were often included in sets of travelling equipment and made in precious or semi-precious metal. To quaff out of something crafted to resemble a lady's leg, complete with garter, might have helped to make palatable some appalling local beverage. Doubtless the slightly rude versions were the sort of thing travellers bought as souvenirs, just as they buy mugs and cups looking like moustache cups or lavatory basins to-day. One can see the stalls catering for the Roman legions, the Crusaders, Marlborough's armies, Nelson's sailors, and hear the comments, 'Rather a comic little thing I picked up last leave – ever so jolly, what? But don't let your good lady see it.'

A similar trend today is the use of chamberpots as drinking vessels. Now that the bedside or 'night' table doesn't contain this any more (nor does the sideboard), it appears that, in addition to being used as cache-pots or flower-pots, the often very pretty china pots of past times are utilised as eggnogg bowls, or even versions of loving cups (see page 24). Travelling toilet sets included smallish pots, which might well be adapted, as christening mugs often are, for the sort of long drink that is an agreeable refresher, such as a punch, mull, or cup; metal chamberpots, of course, could be used for actually heating wine. The most comic use of them, however – and the sort of thing that is both very British and makes the French shake their heads in total inability to understand our supposed sense of humour – occurred as a result of the capture in 1813 by the 14th King's Hussars, now the 14th/20th King's Hussars, of Joseph Bonaparte's carriage after the Battle of Vitoria.

Elizabeth Longford's *Wellington, the years of the sword* (Weidenfeld & Nichol-

'*The Emperor*' *chamberpot. This is the pot taken from the travelling set found in the carriage of Joseph Bonaparte when this was captured after the Battle of Vitoria in 1813. It is now the property of the 14/20th King's Hussars and is used to serve Champagne on special guest nights.*

son 1969) describes how 'Captain Henry Wyndham of the 14th Light Dragoons and Lieutenant Lord Worcester of the 10th Hussars . . . discharged their pistols into the coach's near-side window and out sprang the Intrusive King on the other side . . . possibly it was the magnetic contents of the coach which held back the pursuers. From among the treasures inside, Wyndham's Dragoons acquired Joseph's lordly silver *pot de chambre*, which they christened 'The Emperor'. Their successors still use it at mess functions for drinking toasts in Champagne, after which the pot is placed ceremoniously on the drinker's head.' The regiment thereby got nicknamed 'the Emperor's chambermaids.'

The 'Elgin' glass appears to have been of recent date, but its origin is obscure. On a short stem, it is urn-shaped, both the base of the bowl and its top curving slightly outwards, the bowl itself being two or three times the height of the stem. It is a glass totally unsuitable for the consumption of any wine at all, because the shape makes it impossible to swing the wine around, thereby releasing the bouquet, and the size is such that the measure is mean anyway, even if the glass is filled to the brim, as it is by many catering establishments which should know better. The schooner is merely a larger version of this nasty drinking vessel.

For many years I believed the tag attached to this glass and its name, derived from Thomas Bruce, seventh Earl of Elgin, 1766–1841. This gentleman was he whose name is forever associated with the Elgin Marbles, the subject of a fascinating book, *Lord Elgin and the Marbles* by William St Clair (Oxford University Press 1983). Tradition seems to have had it that this Lord Elgin was a parsimonious man, who had a special glass designed for his use, giving the impression of a more generous measure than it actually contained. Certainly the glass bears out this. It was only when I received a protest from the present Lord Elgin's secretary for promulgating this tradition that I began to investigate its source and certainly there seems to be no foundation for the seventh Earl's reputation as a mean man. True, when fitting out the expedition which was to result in the removal of the Marbles (an expedition which eventually created debts so large that he had to end his days in France to escape his creditors), he did refuse to engage the painter J.M.W. Turner, because Turner asked for a salary of £400 a year, a big retainer in those days. Otherwise, Lord Elgin does not appear to have been tight-fisted and it is a pity that the original order by him to the glass works cannot be amplified with any specifications made at the time. The Elgin glass, however, is somewhat similar to glasses that were in use for toastmasters, who were obliged to limit the amount they consumed and also had to be able to bang the base of the glass on the table to announce the toasts.

Any museum having a section devoted to glassware will probably display some examples of German glasses. The most famous historic glass is the *römer*, which is often referred to in English as 'rummer' although it is nothing whatsoever to do with rum, the name probably coming from a Flemish term. The römer has a shallow bowl, with a ridged foot decorated with several rings, which are sometimes elongated into a fat, ridged stem. Sometimes römers are made of green or yellowish green glass and may have 'prunts', or raised globules on the sides of the stem or on the bowl of the glass, which may have a knob, or knop, on it. The 'raspberry prunts' which decorate many glasses are indeed in shape like halved raspberries applied to the glass.

The 'humpen' glass, particularly associated with Bavaria and Saxony, is in shape rather like a slightly concave barrel without a stem. Very often humpen glasses are elaborately decorated, engraved and even coloured. Very ceremonial – very ostentatious.

These days the most usual glasses for German wines are stemmed, with smallish slightly bulbous bowls; the stem may be of brown glass, which is particularly associated with Rhine wines, while green is associated with wines of the Mosel. In the past, our ancestors would use glasses with tinted bowls so as to conceal the presence of any 'flyers' or bits in the wine, something that is unlikely to offend us today, especially as so many wines are subjected to what some of us find excessive filtration. (Every time a wine goes through a filter, something, in addition to the bits, is removed from it, perhaps to the drinker's loss.)

One traditional glass of this type is known as the 'Treviris', from the Latin form of the name for the City of Trier. This is slightly shallower than the usual type of glass used for German wines and cut with a specific pattern: the indentations and crossings circle the bowl and some of the pattern is repeated on the foot; a knob, usually facetted, sits at the base of the stem. This knob is intended to give a firm hold to the hand. The bowl of the Treviris glass curves slightly inwards; although, to anyone who loves the tissue-thin crystal glasses in which many fine wines are served, cut glass is a little too thick and prominent to the lips, the Treviris shape is certainly elegant and pleasing. If a number of fine Mosel wines is to be served, then the finest wine will be poured into a smaller version of the basic glass shape – which means that the precious liquid (some of such wines may run into treble figures of pounds sterling per bottle) may be shared between as many people as possible for leisurely appraisal.

Wine glasses from about 1765, with colour twist stems. Only a small amount of wine would be contained in them and obviously they were intended for elegant drinking with sips interspersed between polite conversation.

Many regions have glasses of a shape peculiar to them, although in these days a variety of shapes may not always be available from glassworks, which make their profit by turning out vast quantities of ordinary drinking vessels and, of course, bottles – primarily for breweries. Dishwashers don't always easily accommodate certain shapes of glass either.

Glasses used for sparkling wines tend to have a point at the bowl's base, because this makes the rising bubbles look attractive; the Vouvray glass, for example, is also roughly triangular, with a bulge in the middle. In some old pictures, such as those of the great Dutch and Flemish artists, the glass used for sparkling wine is like a tall isosceles triangle standing on its apex. The wine rises along the sides of the triangle.

above right *17th century serpent goblet.*

above far right *English drawn trumpet wine glass, from about 1745–1760, when deep-toned glass was sometimes used for wines.*

below right *15th century goblets from Murano, Venice, decorated with enamel.*

below *Sir Godfrey Kneller (1646–1723) shows the 7th Earl of Lincoln and the 1st Duke of Newcastle enjoying a glass of wine – note that they hold their glasses by the foot in the approved style – poured from a somewhat common-looking wicker-bound flask.*

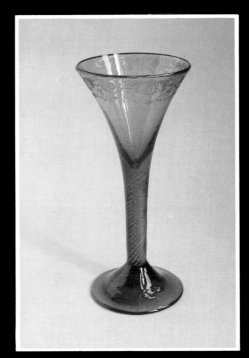

MATUSALEN 1ª
WAS
DEDICATED
TUSALEM
HE RT HON SIR
WINSTON CHURCHILL
K.G. O.M. C.H. M.P.
IN HONOUR OF HIS
80 TH BIRTHDAY
Martin Luther
US NAVY
10/11/55
12-2-68
26-X-29

Some old Champagne glasses have hollow stems, so that the wine goes from the cup of the bowl right down to the foot; they are delightful to use but awkward to keep clean and bright. In some sets of antique glassware, especially of the 19th century, the bowl of the glass is fitted into an ornate holder which is of precious metal. This type of drinking vessel is known as a zarf – a useful word, as my informant told me, when playing Scrabble. A great jeweller designed a contemporary version of the zarf in a set of cut-glass bowls that could be screwed on to a gold or silver gilt base – practical in case you broke the glass, which could then be replaced (at impressive cost).

What with the thickness of the cut-glass bowl and the value of the base, I, invited to the launch of these admittedly elegant vessels, was rather inhibited about enjoying the Champagne therein.

It seems a pity, however, that designers of glassware today have done so little to enliven the basic shapes. They tend merely to vary the cutting – which could as well be on the stem or foot of the glass, leaving the bowl free for the drinker to see the wine's colour. They often distort the shape of the glass so that the rim turns back and the wine tends to dribble from your lips as you drink; or produce a bowl otherwise unsuitable in shape for the straightforward appreciation of fine wines – enjoyed like other pleasures, 'naked', without the distractions of cutting, engraving, convolutions and, certainly, any colouring.

Sherry drawn from the butt. In the background note cask heads inscribed by distinguished visitors, or as with that bearing Churchill's name, dedicated on a special occasion.

Parcel-gilt cup, dating from 1493, of surprisingly pure design and almost modern appearance.

The most beautiful 20th century glasses I have ever seen were made by the great artist in glass, Lalique: he was a native of Champagne and Madame Cathérine Taittinger, displaying them, told me her father had commissioned them from Lalique. Each has a deepish bowl, incurving at the rim, on a very tall stem; the colourless glass bowl is lightly engraved with the face of the famous smiling angel from the façade of the Cathedral at Reims, so that, as you tilt the glass, the angel appears between you and the wine, benevolently enigmatic.

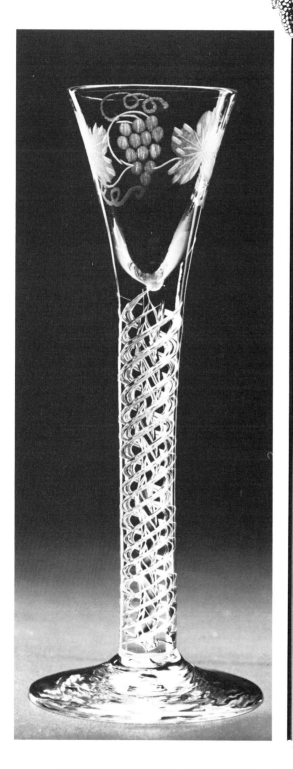

ntique glasses with minute
bowls, often on intricately
patterned tall stems, were
generally intended for
cordials. The word itself relates to the
Latin for heart, *cor*, signifying very
strong drink, which was frequently
served when the gentlemen staggered
upstairs to the drawing-room, after a
long session in the dining-room, needing
the equivalent of a pick-me-up when
they joined the ladies. The cordial,
although it could be pleasant, was in the
nature of a medicinal beverage.

Solitaires

mong other adjuncts to wine
and its service are solitaires,
which many people may
have seen and not recog-
nised, supposing them to be finger
bowls. But the solitaire is slightly deeper
than the ordinary finger bowl and will
have either one or two lips; this is so that
a glass may be inserted, upended, resting
on the lip by its stem, and rinsed in the
water in the solitaire, thereby enabling a
single glass – the 'sole one' – to be used
for several different wines. Sometimes a
vessel of this sort was also used to cool
glasses, especially in the days when the
hectic and prolonged hard drinking sessions made any cold beverage particularly welcome.

*Cordial glass, from about 1750, trumpet-
shaped, with a representation of a vine with
grapes and stem with spiral threads.*

❧ Coolers ❧

But the most usual type of wine coolers are the gigantic, baby-bath-sized vessels, often very elaborate examples of the silversmith's art, which used to be placed in the middle of the table. They were used to cool the wine bottles as well as the glasses. The ice house, where blocks of ice could be kept throughout the year for the enhancement of various dishes and drinks, was a standard fixture in many great houses of former days.

right English or Irish glass wine cooler, of about 1815–1820. The various sections can be taken apart, according to the height of the bottle to be cooled. The whole is somewhat monstrous, demonstrating how the cutter's art is here displayed superbly – but adding nothing either by practicality or charm to the huge ostentatious piece.

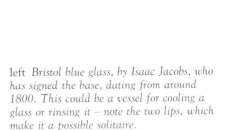

left Bristol blue glass, by Isaac Jacobs, who has signed the base, dating from around 1800. This could be a vessel for cooling a glass or rinsing it – note the two lips, which make it a possible solitaire.

One distinctive type of cooler is known as a 'Monteith'. It is said to have been evolved in the 17th century by a Scottish gentleman; as he wore a scalloped coat and the scooped-out indentations around the rim of the cooler were similar, it acquired his name. The indentations served to hold the feet of the glasses, so that the bowls of the glasses hung down into the ice or ice and water.

Monteith, silver-gilt, 1709. The rim of the bowl can be removed – presumably for easier cleaning. In 1683 Anthony à Wood wrote 'This year . . . came up a vessel or bason notched at the brims to let drinking glasses hang there by the feet so that the body or drinking place might hang in the water to coole them. Such a bason was called a "Monteith", from a fantastical Scot called "Monsieur Monteith" who at that time or a little before wore the bottoms of his cloake or coats so notched.'

18th century glass tun, decorated with a cockerel on the spigot and Bacchus on a mini-cask above the bunghole.

🍇 Accessories 🍇

Any display of small antique silverware or items in silvergilt will probably include many of the adjuncts to the service of the mixed drinks so popular in former times, when the wine might be of such 'ordinary' quality that additions, in the form of spices, herbs and honey could but improve the drink. Small-scale grinders for spice and graters for nutmegs might be part of the equipment carried about by the gourmet of former times, very much as a contemporary counterpart may pack antacid tablets and dental floss before undertaking a gastronomic voyage. There are graters for paring down hunks of sugar (before

it came in lumps), small knives for peeling or slicing fruit, similar to the individual fruit knives carried as recently as my own father's day, whippy-handled ladles for punch, made of whalebone before whales became scarce and protected – these last often with a lip to facilitate the pouring of hot liquid, for punch could be hot or cold.

Among miniature glassware you may find the odd toddy lifter, a globular-ended rod with a hole in the globe as well as the top; this would be plunged into the punch or cup, so that the liquid filled

the globular part of the vessel. Then, with the thumb stopping the aperture at the top, the lifter could be removed from the punch bowl and, by the holder manipulating his thumb, the liquid would be directed from the globular end into the glass or goblet. The liquid does not run out while the thumb remains over the top of the lifter.

A similar, but somewhat larger device is used to siphon off samples of wine from a cask for tasting; it is known as a *pipette* or *velenche*. You insert it, so that the wine fills the body of the pipette (which is often glass, but sometimes metal), then, as you withdraw the instrument from the wine, you put your thumb over the top opening and, by manipulating the pressure, direct the wine from the other end into glasses or tasting cups. It is quite easy to do. In the Cognac region samples of spirit are drawn from the cask by a small metal cup on the end of a wire, which is called *une preuve* or, sometimes, a 'thief'.

1828 punch ladle, with medallions in the bowl. Various types of punch were prepared according to the season or specific occasion and many well-known clubs and eating-places in the UK and US gave their names to their particular recipes for punch.

In Hungary, where the conservation casks are enormous, a large-scale and peculiar version of the pipette or velenche is used. This is called a *lopo*. It is a hollow rod the length of a walking stick or even longer, with a quite large bulbous vessel at the top, capable of holding the contents of a bottle; this is sometimes elaborately decorated with glassy 'frills' and it is wide enough at its maximum width to avoid the risk of slipping from the holder's grasp and sliding into the cask through the bung hole. The wine is drawn up into it by being sucked through the long tube, considerable lung power being necessary for the cellarman to pull out sufficient wine. When the vessel is full, the man who has pulled the sample puts the lopo over his shoulder, the better to support its weight.

Drawing a cask sample in a chai, or above ground store of wine in the Pomerol region of Bordeaux, using the velenche. The red wine, foaming up in the early stages after going into the Bordeaux barriques, overflows and pours out through the bunghole. Note the cane-bound barriques intended for maturation in the chai. 'Barriques de transport', used for sending out wine in bulk, are, these days, bound with metal for strength.

left *Tasting wine in the Beaujolais, the glass velenche directed into the irregularly indented tastevin.*

The venenciador displaying his skill in directing the sherry from over his head into the separate copitas held in his right hand, without letting a drop fall to the floor. The flexible whalebone handle of the venencia makes the process even more difficult.

right *Gilt wager cup, bearing the arms of the Goldsmiths' Company and the engraved arms of Francis Boone Thomas, Prime Warden in 1881. The lady, in Elizabethan dress, holds the small swivel cup above her head between two oak branches. It dates from 1829.*

Cask samples in the sherry region of Spain, however, are drawn by manipulating a device called a *venencia*. This is a metal cup on the end of a pliable whalebone handle, which has a rounded hook, rather like that of a coathanger, on its end. This hook will catch on to the side of the bunghole if the person drawing the sample drops the venencia. The metal cup will go straight through any *flor*, the odd fluffy growth that forms on the surface of certain sherries, without disturbing it. The venencia of Sanlúcar de Barrameda is slightly different, made of bamboo, the cup on the end being also of bamboo, hollowed-out and blocked at the base. I suppose that, in former times, the wine makers here may have found this easier to manipulate, or perhaps the usual venencia was just too expensive; both the metal cup and the whalebone are quite costly and a real venencia is a prized possession. The late General Franco and the late head of Williams & Humbert were each presented with a solid gold venencia. I was allowed to borrow the latter for photographing years ago – it was not only beautiful but could have been put to use immediately.

The wielder of the venencia can indulge in even more displays of skill than the person drinking from the porrón: the instrument can be whirled around without any of the wine being spilled and a real expert will direct the glittering arc of sherry into a whole clutch of glasses held in his other hand without a drop going on the floor. Each sherry bodega has its champion and there is, or was, one master at Domecq who would hold fourteen glasses between the fingers of his left hand while pouring the wine from high in the air behind his head. As with spitting, it must take a lot of preliminary practice in secret.

Sometimes a museum may display a wager cup, a representation of a girl in a full-skirted long dress, arms extended above her head to hold a small vessel like a tub on a swivel. When bets were being placed, one had to drink from the contents of the small vessel while upending the woman's figure, then the full skirt would receive a second helping of wine and the procedure would be reversed. All vaguely pornographic and I admit I have never seen the trick achieved or even attempted, though I am assured that it can be done.

Certain fat jugs, usually in majolica in their original form, have become known as *Bellarmines*. They seem to have been a speciality of the Rhineland in the late 16th century, although they were subsequently made in vast quantities in England and used for ale and sack in taverns. They are supposed to be representative of Cardinal Bellarmine (1542–1621) a native of Tuscany, fond of all the good things of life and showing this in his figure. Some of the examples show a bearded, plump masculine face on the side of the jug. It is easy to see how a vessel of this kind could be adapted, featuring topical personalities, and it still exists today in the form of the Toby jug, often showing the faces of caricatured personalities.

The tankard or mug type of drinking vessel of former times, made in somewhat haphazard sizes according to the individual measures of the potter, silversmith or craftsman in pewter, often had small stud-like pegs inside, each of these indicating the amount of liquid in a particular measure. This is the origin of the expression 'to drink a peg', the current equivalent being a glass with the official mark on it, or the measure that must be displayed by those selling drink for consumption on their premises.

The Tantalus of Victorian times, consisting of several glass decanters in a frame which could be locked so that the vessels could not be broached at will – albeit showing the temptations they contained – is probably familiar to many. But some of the silver or metal wine labels that are often suspended from the decanter necks bear names that may not be known nowadays. Perhaps the most usual is 'Nig', which of course is merely the word gin in reverse, supposedly intended to mislead Victorian servants; but some antique examples of these wine labels bear names totally unfamiliar to drinkers of our time. (See page 65.)

Modern examples of labels usually merely give the generic name of the wine – sherry, Champagne, claret and so on – but there is another type of decanter neck decoration, which I do not think has existed for very long: this consists of a chain with a prong or small fork-like protuberance at each end, on which the cork of the bottle of wine can be impaled, the chain then being hung round the decanter for people to inspect the cork if they so wish. Sometimes the prongs are attached to a representation of a vine leaf.

Labels

The subject of wine labels is a big one. Several notable collections of antique examples are on display at the present time, of which that in the Wine Museum of John Harvey of Bristol is perhaps the most famous and easily accessible. It may surprise people to know that it is only recently that the paper label has been a regular part of the 'dressing' of the bottle. In former times there were occasional instances of parchment labels or, even, paper ones; there were also tags of ivory, bone or wood hung on bottles, much as the silver ones were hung around decanter necks in the dining-room as early as the 18th century. But the bottles in the cellars were not labelled – indeed, in the cellars of the great producers even today bottles are not invariably labelled until they are about to be offered for sale; a nice damp cellar, which is what wine likes, may cause labels to deteriorate over a long period and the stock can be identified by the bin number.

In his superb Book of the Wine Label (published by Home and Van Thal 1947), N.M. Penzer cites as examples parchment labels represented in an engraving of Hogarth's An Election Entertainment, 1755. But Penzer is definite that, whereas parchment labels were used at this time, the silver 'Bottle Ticket' or, as we should say, decanter label, was for the use of drinkers at home. When the private cellars of great houses were established it was obviously necessary to sort out what was where; a bin label, referring to the contents, was hung on the bin. This could be related to

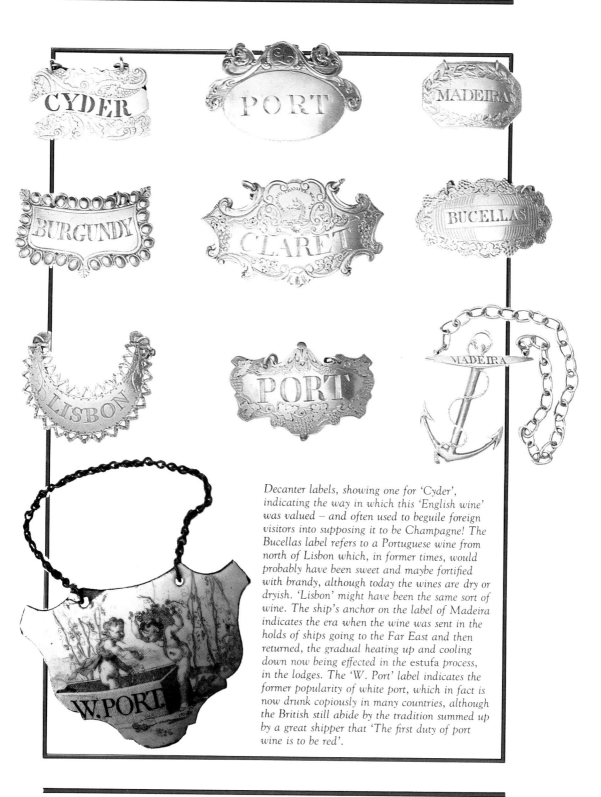

Decanter labels, showing one for 'Cyder', indicating the way in which this 'English wine' was valued – and often used to beguile foreign visitors into supposing it to be Champagne! The Bucellas label refers to a Portuguese wine from north of Lisbon which, in former times, would probably have been sweet and maybe fortified with brandy, although today the wines are dry or dryish. 'Lisbon' might have been the same sort of wine. The ship's anchor on the label of Madeira indicates the era when the wine was sent in the holds of ships going to the Far East and then returned, the gradual heating up and cooling down now being effected in the estufa process, in the lodges. The 'W. Port' label indicates the former popularity of white port, which in fact is now drunk copiously in many countries, although the British still abide by the tradition summed up by a great shipper that 'The first duty of port wine is to be red'.

the cellar book, kept by the butler or steward.

Special re-usable bottles bearing their personal seal or some distinguishing mark – usually on a lozenge on the shoulder of the bottle – were provided for such wine merchants' customers as could afford them.

On October 23rd, 1663, Samuel Pepys writes, 'To Mr Rawlinson's, and saw some of my new bottles being made, with my crest upon them, filled with wine, about five or six dozen'. Some innkeepers also appear to have ordered their own marked bottles, so that customers could take them home – a form of advertising anticipating the

plastic carrier bag – when only small quantities were required at a time. The important thing to remember is that the actual name of the wine was never marked on this lozenge, seal or stamp, only the name of the customer. Therefore some further form of identification as to the wine was necessary. Hence the bottle label, to indicate the contents.

There are members of the wine trade still living who have informed me that, except for certain very fine and famous wines, their ancestral firms would have merely supplied, upon request, so many dozen of 'X and Co's claret and Burgundy or port'. The wines might be given paper labels when they were to be despatched to the customer, but some-

times they were not. A pleasant development of the personalised bottle occurs today in the revival of certain older bottle shapes, sometimes even with a seal on the shoulder, by some firms associated with classic wines. But of course, there are no hand-blown bottles today and the weight of an old bottle, as compared with its modern version, is striking.

For certain of the great Quinta do Noval ports a bottle with a little indentation, almost like a lip at the rim, is used; I once asked Fernando van Zeller, whose family owns the quinta, why this was so, and was informed that it was because, in former times, this 'lip' was where the bottle would be broken off from the blower's glass rod. The tradition has been maintained, although today the bottles are moulded, not blown.

It is perhaps relevant to note that bottles referred to as 'shot' bottles in relation to port, are those which, in former times, would be filled up with small shot, which was then shaken up so that the new bottle would be slightly pitted inside, thereby enabling the crust of a vintage port to form and cling firmly. Sometimes, I believe, old-established wine merchants still arrange for such old bottles, especially large sizes, to be used for bottling special consignments of very fine wine (such as those reserved for their own luncheon rooms). But I do not know whether their use results in a superior quality of wine, especially now that vintage port is bottled in Portugal and is therefore not subject to the variations that were inevitable when different merchants in the UK did their own bottling.

Bottles, with seals indicating the owners, with dates. Did the people ordering specify a particular shape – or did it depend on the glass blower? Note the way that these bottles could not have been laid on their sides, for long-term maturation of the wine, so that it was only with the evolution of the longer, straight-sided bottle, that wines able to improve with keeping could be put into them – wine-making techniques were probably adapted as a result and the great period of long-lived wines for laying down began.

🍇 Corkscrews 🍇

The device whereby the cork is pulled out of the bottle is nowadays known as the corkscrew. It has a literature of its own and collectors of antique corkscrews (oh, those corkscrews with brushes that I threw away when clearing out my grandparents' effects!) and societies all over the world are devoted to their history and assembly.

It is thought by the authorities Bernard M. Watney and Homer D. Babbage in *Corkscrews for Collectors* (Sotheby Parke Bernet 1981) that the first reference to a 'Steel Worme used for drawing Corks out of Bottles' was in 1681, but it may well have been that people who made wine, whether from grapes or other fruits, berries and vegetables, had earlier evolved some device for taking out the cork – unless it was actually blown out by the process of fermentation, before this was fully understood. Here I speak with personal experience, for when I was an infant my parents had a garden in which there were various fruit trees, many of them damsons. My mother, a good cook in the English tradition and my father, son of an Oxfordshire and Gloucestershire farming family, decided to attempt making damson wine. (Already there were bottled damsons, damson jam, damson jelly – Mummie would never have thought of pickling damsons, alas!)

What my parents did when making the wine I certainly can't remember, but a dark crimson liquid went into bottles and, at once, the corks were tied down. (Daddy could tie down Champagne corks expertly, as I learned twenty years later.) The bottles were arranged in the

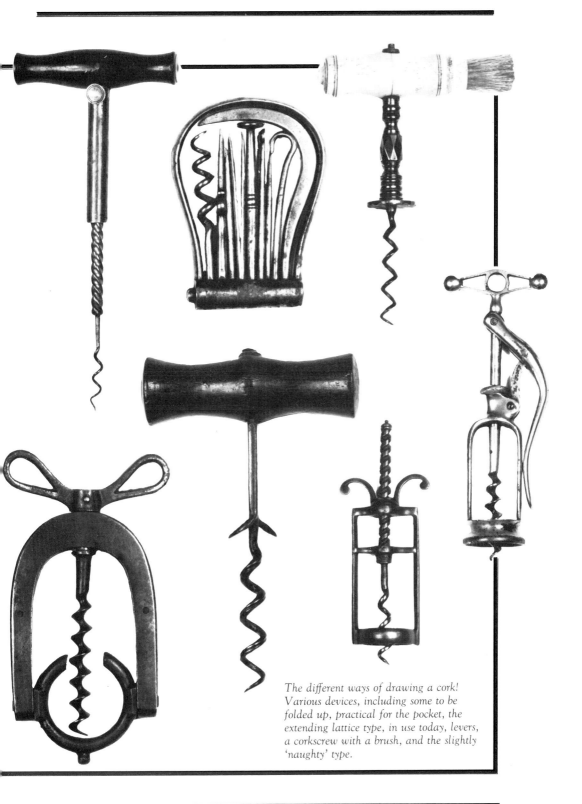

The different ways of drawing a cork!
Various devices, including some to be
folded up, practical for the pocket, the
extending lattice type, in use today, levers,
a corkscrew with a brush, and the slightly
'naughty' type.

corridor of our flat, along the top of mother's cottage piano. A few days later I, aged about three, was trotting past when my footfall started a series of explosions. At that age one is not astonished by anything. But I can still remember going into the drawing-room, vaguely uncomfortable because sticky – and everyone screaming and leaping towards me in horror – as I appeared to be covered in blood. (The piano was a total loss.)

In 1686, one Claver Morris, a Devonshire doctor, bought a 'Corkdrawer' but he used this for cider. The 'bottle screw' seems to have begun as a fairly simple device, such as might be carried in the pocket: a ring with a spiral depending from it. Of course, corks were not necessarily all of the same length, so that the length of the screw of your cork extractor depended on the wine you were opening or likely to open. The brush, incidentally, that is part of some corkscrews that may be found around today, was for brushing away the cracked wax over the cork, as wax was used to seal the corks of many bottles of wine before the metal capsule came into universal acceptance (and before the loathsome plastic capsule, which is supposed to be, and seldom is, easily ripped away). Anyone who has banged the wax off an historic bottle and watched the bits shower wildly around, will appreciate the practicality of the brush.

The ingenuity of the makers of corkscrews would seem to have no end. There are variations of successful types continually coming onto the market. Some

are quite complex mechanisms. Some may incorporate a decanting device, so that the bottle can be tilted when the cork has been extracted and the wine poured, without risk of sediment affecting the limpidity of the drink.

I have a device which fits over the neck of a sparkling wine bottle and then claws up the cork, which cannot fly; I have grippers that will hold the 'mushroom' top of a bottle of sparkling wine (made by the Champagne method), so that, as you correctly turn the bottle *not* the cork, the mushroom is firmly held in the grippers and, as the instinct is to grip tighter when the cork begins to move, the cork is held as it comes out. As far as I know, this useful device is only available to those who are friends of Colmans of Norwich (who market Veuve du Vernay). There is even a version that will grip the top of a plastic sparkling wine stopper and enable this too to be extracted safely.

But, unless you are able to crack off the neck of a bottle, either with hot tongs or with the proverbial upward flick of the wrist – and if so I should recommend some form of filtration, in case splinters of glass get into the wine – there is another method of cork extraction. It does not involve the more usual method of pushing a recalcitrant cork down into the wine and then carefully (preferably with a wooden skewer or some similar long instrument that is not metal) holding back the cork until the wine can be poured past it.

The procedure is that you take the capsule off a bottle of wine in which,

Mick Morris drawing a sample of wine in Rutherglen, Victoria, Australia. ('Down under' even the pipette or velenche is somewhat larger and longer than in the northern hemisphere!)

Using the lopo to draw samples and put them into glasses in a cellar in Hungary.

preferably, there is no great deposit likely to be disturbed. Then, cushioning the bottle on something soft, hold it horizontally against a wall or something equally solid. Proceed to bang the base of the bottle gently and progressively against the wall, so that the continual shocks will impel the emergence of the cork by pushing out the wine and air inside. It may take time – but I have seen it work. (But it would probably be simpler and safer to push the cork in.)

Tasting Cups

Most people will have seen a wine waiter with a chain around his neck, from which is suspended a shallow silver cup. This is a tastevin, although its use in public in the modern restaurant is something of a gimmick, to attract attention and give the drinker an impression of something special being ceremonially presented. In fact, the sommelier does not always use it and, when a glass is available, this is far better suited to an on-the-spot appraisal of a freshly opened wine in a good light.

In past times, however, the traveller and, certainly, anyone engaged in the wine trade, would invariably carry his own form of tasting cup about with him. Drinking vessels of wood, horn, pottery, or even semi-precious or precious metals might not be particularly clean in inns and certainly not easily available in cellars; nor is the ordinary beaker shape ideal for appraising a wine's colour. When a sample was drawn from the cask, only a small quantity of wine was required at a time; and in the cellars of small peasant growers only a small quantity might have been available.

The history of the tasting cup is long. Shallow, decorated cups in pottery have been found in Knossos in Crete and in Argos, dating from as long ago as 1100 BC; others in bronze, found in Etruscan tombs in Rome, date from the 15th century BC. In the house of the Vettii in Pompei there is a fresco showing *amorini* as wine merchants, which is thought to be the very first representation of serious tasting: the amorini are receiving the

Louis XV silver partly-fluted tastevin, dating from about 1735, showing St. Charles (probably St. Charles Borromeo, 1538–1584). The handle, in the form of a serpent, is an interesting survival of the association of the snake, shown in the caduceus borne by physicians, as a mysterious and somehow sacred creature involved with wine.

above left *Sampling the freshly made nouveau from the press in the Beaujolais – everybody concerned will have 'purple-stained mouths' for days.*

below left *The sardine fishing fleet refreshing themselves from a wicker-covered large bottle aboard ship – the cushioning of the container with straw or wickerwork is a very old tradition.*

The tastevin in action in Burgundy, the irregular indentations showing up the colour of the wine and the shape of the cup presenting the wine so that it hits the mouth more widely than occurs with a glass. In the past, most people actively involved with wine would have carried their own. Madame Clicquot's small, plain tastevin, for example, is preserved in the firm's collection of treasures.

wine poured from an amphora into a shallow cup, one of them then offering a sample to a potential buyer. Every one of these tasting cups, most of them with a loop or handle, so that the cup could be held steady and, if required, suspended on a cord, could be utilised by tasters today. The shape has changed little. The decoration, however, varies according to the period: grapes, vine leaves, coats of arms and mottos, representations of Bacchus and entwined serpents forming the border or handle are only some of the variations that may be found in examples that have survived. The serpent motif may be a survivor of the association of the snake form with Aesculapius, the God of Medicine, wine being highly esteemed as a medicament in ancient times and, indeed, until recently.

In his magnificent history of tastevins, *Le Tastevin à travers les siècles* (Editions des 4 Seigneurs, Grenoble 1977) René Mazenot lists a number of different forms or names of the tastevin; he also points out that a similar tasting cup was in use for cider. The form in which people today are most familiar with the tastevin is the Burgundy type, in which the interior has a number of indentations, grooves and bulges, usually irregularly arranged, so that, as the wine runs over these, its colour may be clearly appraised; even today in a cellar in Burgundy, where the tasting may be preliminarily conducted before the wines are tried again in the tasting-room, there may be very little light, and that possibly only from a bulb of low power suspended in the ceiling, or even a candle. So any help in seeing ·the colour of the wine, white or red, is useful.

In the Bordeaux region, however, tasting is first done in the chai, which is the wine store above ground; it is not possible to excavate underground cellars in many areas here, because of the water table. So the Bordeaux *tasse à vin* is a plain cup, with one bulge in the middle of it, over which the wine can run as the cup is tilted. A saucer, similar in shape to the tasse à vin, but made of white enamel or white porcelain and known as a *tomboladero* is used by the port trade, in which the colour of the wine is of enormous importance.

Tapas

Tapas are the small quantities of nuts, crisps, olives or more substantial food-stuffs – meat-balls, fishballs, hot sausages, and savouries on toast *ad infinitum*, which are traditional accompaniments to a drink ordered in Spain. Indeed, if you are able to circulate in some chic areas, the tapas accompanying even a single glass of wine may well provide the first course of a meal. (And, those who have been hungry inform me, a scratch repast may be made from these 'nibbles'.) Tapas may well have their origin in the Mediterranean tradition, which survives to this day, that drink is not served without something to eat. At one time, certainly, in Cyprus and, I imagine, in Greece, a drink would always arrive accompanied by one or more saucers of nuts, little biscuits, chunks of cheese, slivers of radish, slices of the local salami; unfortunately, economic pressures make this custom less usual today, although the principle of not drinking without eating is sound.

But the word tapa actually means 'cover'. I am assured, by several friends in the wine trade, that there were until recently – at least in London – some sherry bars where the copita glass of sherry would be presented to the customer with a flat biscuit laid over the top. This 'cover' provided the suitable 'blotting paper' for the drink. Even after World War II, in some bars in London where sherry, Madeira and port were served by the glass (not yet wine by the glass, a more recent innovation) there would be a large fruit cake standing on the bar and customers could order a slice of this as an accompaniment to whatever they were drinking.

Asking for 'an octave' in a public house or bar, is a very old-fashioned way of ordering sherry which I have never observed. Eight different sherries, each in a separate glass, would be presented in response. Obviously, some time was required by customers ordering an octave to get through the sherries. But probably those who asked for an octave had an amplitude of time. The sherries would range from very dry to sweet, or sweetish. Possibly a couple of friends or even three people would share the drinking. It seems odd that, in these days when anything that promotes a commodity is exploited, sometimes rather shrilly, the notion of the octave has never been revived.

Another device, peculiar to the Rheinpfalz or Palatinate region of Germany, is the 'carousel'. This is a wrought-iron turntable, with spaces on the circle for six, eight or even a dozen glasses to be slipped in, the spaces sometimes bearing numbers alongside.

A different wine is poured into each glass and then the carousel is carried in its frame to the table where the drinkers await it: they turn it round, sampling each wine – remember, these are not necessarily very big-bellied glasses – and a good time is had by all. The practice enables people to sample several local wines (for these may be the 'open' or carafe wines of the area) at moderate cost. Again, I've never understood why wine bars elsewhere haven't adopted the admirable idea. Or are drinkers hesitant about sharing glasses in these ultra-hygienic times? (See page 45 as to the efficacy of wine as a disinfectant.)

It is pertinent to remember that, in the 19th century, when the man of the house returned from his desk in the City he and his lady wife would take a glass of wine together, sometimes Madeira, sometimes Marsala, accompanied by a slice of cake, before dressing for dinner. Working hours were much longer then and this fare would have been both acceptable and reviving to someone who certainly did not have afternoon tea at his desk, or maybe even much lunch. Bear in mind that the preprandial cocktail or drink at home is a very recent innovation; even right up to 1939 many households would not have offered one as routine: Barbara Cartland, in her autobiography *We Danced All Night* (Hutchinson 1971), says that drinks were not offered before meals in the 1920s; if a man wanted a drink, he sought out the butler and she says that 'even in 1937, in my father-in-law's house, if I wanted a glass of sherry before dinner my husband had to fetch it for me up to my bedroom'.

It should be remembered that, in those days, it was possible for everyone to arrive on time for an evening meal: this would have been prepared by staff in the kitchen, so that, when the mistress of the house greeted her guests, she had only to introduce them to each other, tell them who was to go into dinner with whom and wait, probably for no more than a quarter of an hour, to be told that 'Dinner is served'. The preprandial drink, which, in many continental countries might have been taken in the café or bar by the man of the house on his way home, certainly did not become general until after World War II; even then women might often refuse a drink before a meal should it be offered. Uncertainty about when people can arrive and the fact that the hostess probably has to do the cooking have extended the preprandial drinks.

To this day, visitors invited to many French households, or households in countries where domestic staff are easier to find, even for middle class establishments, may find that they are not offered a drink before they go into dinner. The long sessions of postprandial drinking, of course, have been dealt a blow by the campaign against drinking and driving (or even walking or waddling home with uncertain gait) after a vast consumption of alcohol. So, when you see one of the long menus – each course accompanied by a different wine – that survive from a hundred years ago, remind yourself that diners on these occasions might not have had anything to drink beforehand – and would have had no problems about getting themselves home later on.

Varieties of vin

Wine is a wonderful, mysterious thing. It isn't a mere drink — nor is its quality definable (little wonder that wines are so often likened to people). The very word vin *seems to excite the imagination of makers and drinkers. Most people today will be at least vaguely aware of* nouveau *wine as vintage time comes round; this was first associated with Beaujolais, but is now being made in many other regions of France and, as* novello, *in Italy. It is also rushed from the antipodes to such export markets as enjoy sampling a novelty, in the sense that the wine is new, young, fresh.*

Of course, if a *nouveau* or *primeur* type of wine, able to be consumed at least within months, maybe weeks, of its vintage can be produced, and if, at the same time, a demand has been created sufficient to sell the wine within a short while, both the producer and the customer will be satisfied. It is also true that the publicity attracted by such 'new' wines does draw many people to sample them who might otherwise not have thought of doing so – if they then continue to drink wine, then this is all to the good.

There are endless variations in the production of nouveau. Essentially, the wine is bottled when its immediate or 'first' fermentation has finished and the turbulence of the process, while the wine yeasts act upon the natural sugar in the grapejuice, has died down. The grapejuice or 'must' has now been transformed into wine. So much more is known today about the science involved with wine-making that this stage can be carefully controlled, supervised – and, if need be, protected from any infection or contamination: the wine doesn't 'just happen'.

This is important because, even though the yeasts cease to work in the

The juice from recently crushed grapes is somewhat sludge-like, as in this shot of 'must' in a Saumur cellar.

wine when the cold weather comes, they will usually get going again in the spring. It is then that wine still in cask, vat, or tank will complete its fermentation. Though the new wine is already in bottle, the 'working' of the yeasts may cause complications, pushing out the corks or even bursting bottles as the pressure inside caused by the carbon dioxide gas given off increases. Makers of nouveau should, therefore, guard against this, by so treating the wine prior to bottling that it is unlikely to start 'working' come the spring after the vintage.

There is, however, nothing truly 'new' about nouveau wine. Its drinkers are reverting to the drinking habits of their ancestors, who, before wine was able to be matured in bottle, rushed to drink the first shipments of the new wine. The 'Ban', or proclamation of the vintage – *Ban des vendanges* – was announced so that grape picking might start; thus growers would not be tempted to lower the quality by picking early and making sour wine from unripe grapes. The ships waiting in the port of Bordeaux to be loaded with the casks would subsequently speed up the Gironde estuary to the various ports in England and the Low Countries where they were going to unload and sell their wine, racing in very much the same way as the great grain clippers raced across the oceans in more recent times. In the Port of London, the 'King's Butler' – *Bouteiller* – would go down to sample the cargoes and have first pick of the new wine. Taverns and inns would hang up garlands of green foliage, signifying the arrival of the delicious new vintage, as is done outside Vienna today, when people frequent the *weinstube* for the *heurige* wine. Word would soon get round, before the garland was hung up, that 'It's come!' – hence the saying 'Good wine needs no bush'. Anybody who has drunk the juice of the grapes as it flows stickily from the press will know how pleasant it is: in some wine regions at vintage time it is served with the new season's walnuts. (Beware, though, if you do have the chance of such a sampling. As Shakespeare says, the drink can be 'searching' and, quaffed in quantity, it can set up an unpleasant fermentation inside you.)

New wine was in immediate demand and the ships carrying it would be looked for in the export markets. Pirates who lived on the French coast, in the wilds of the Vendée and along the Channel, watched for the wine fleet each autumn, hoping for loot; because of this, some of the ships carrying the new wine began also to carry arms and fighting men as a defence. This is supposed to be the origin of the Royal Navy.

What is definite, and also dates from these times, is that the mighty *tonne*, a gigantic cask no longer in use, was used as the measure of capacity for the Bordeaux wine fleet. A vessel could transport so many tonnes, or casks of wine. To this day, a ship's capacity is measured in terms of 'tonnage'.

There are many variations on *vin*, sometimes the suffix giving it a specific meaning. For example, *vin clair* is the young wine of Champagne, prior to bottling.

'Le Beaujolais nouveau est arrivé!' proclaim the posters in Paris restaurants and cafés, with the staff often dressed up to celebrate the event as soon as the wine is released in late November.

Vin de consommation courante means wine for everyday drinking; a *vin de garde* is a wine worth keeping for improvement in bottle; a *vin de marque* is a wine bearing a brand name; a *vin ordinaire* is literally 'an ordinary wine' – adequate but no more; a *vin de presse* is a wine made after the initial wine has been drawn off the press and the remaining débris has been subjected to pressing; the result, therefore, is not of prime quality and may be sent for distillation or, if it is drinkable, kept for domestic consumption.

Vin de table and *vin de pays* are official categories of French wines, subjected to certain controls; these days they can be very good. *Vin doux naturel* is a wine from the South of France, of which the Muscats, such as Muscat de Beaumes de Venise, are perhaps the best known;

they are slightly higher than table wine in strength. *Vin de paille*, a term meaning 'straw wine', is a wine made from grapes which have been either laid out on straw mats after picking, or else hung up on frames, so that they dry and shrink somewhat before they go to the press; wines of this kind are made in a number of countries and tend to have a concentration of flavour. They are usually sweeter than most table wines.

Vin jaune is the yellow wine of the Jura region of France, which is left in cask for several years without being topped up, and acted upon by the special bacteria *Mycoderma vini*, which forms the *voile*, or veil on the surface. This phenomenon was noted by Louis Pasteur, a native of the Jura region. His knowledge of this odd wine was a contributory factor to his discovery of the action of bacteria.

Vin sauvage is a sparkling wine made in the Gers region of south-east France; it is violently foaming, somewhat similar to the *vin fou* of the Jura region, which is sparkling because the wine is bottled at the peak of the first period of its fermentation. Italy's *vin santo*, however, is more varied: it is made in a number of regions, is sometimes dry, but perhaps more generally sweetish or definitely sweet. Sometimes the grapes are dried on mats before pressing. It has been suggested that the wine gets its name because the drying of the grapes, which concentrates the juice, sometimes lasts from the period when they are picked in the autumn until just before Easter of the following year, but this is disputed. It is certainly nothing to do with communion wine; nor is it related to the *vin de messe* – found in Tunisia – which appears to be a term of approbation, signifying high quality, but has nothing to do with ecclesiastical usage.

Among general terms applied to *vin* is *vin de tête*, which implies that the wine has been made from the first pressing, or pressings, of the grapes; as these – or, even better, the juice which starts flowing through the weight of the piled up grapes – make the finest wine, the term signifies quality, although it does not appear to have any legal significance. The expression *tête de cuvée* is similarly vague in implication – it should mean superior quality, but this may well depend on who made the wine.

The term *vin de liqueur* has been the subject of much argument in the EEC. To the French, the term 'fortified wine', translated as *un vin fortifié*, implies that the wine has been *viné*, or increased in strength by the straightforward addition of alcohol, which is illegal. So France wished the term *vin de liqueur* to apply to wines such as port, sherry, Madeira and Marsala, which of course are made by the addition of spirit and are as strictly controlled as any French wine. One can imagine the total confusion which would have resulted in the English-speaking world had the term *vin de liqueur* been enforced. The French term for a wine in which the fermentation has been stopped by adding spirit is *vin muté*, but you are not likely to be easily understood if you ask for this in a French bar when you want a glass of port, (*porto*) of which the French nowadays drink far more (of ordinary quality) than the British. The use of the term *vin de liqueur* by the French is somewhat similar to the use of the word claret by the British: most of the rest of the world says 'red Bordeaux', but we won that battle of nomenclature in Brussels, so that, at least in the UK, red Bordeaux is still known as claret. (After all, the English crown did own the Bordeaux region for 299 years! See pages 85–6.)

The most famous variation on *vin* is probably *vin blanc cassis*. The drink originated in Burgundy, where it was made with the dry white Aligoté wine, plus cassis, the blackcurrant liqueur, for which the region is famous. Today the drink is made with all kinds of wine all over France, according to what may be available. The requisite to me is a fairly hard wine, high in acidity. I have known people make the drink with more delicate white wine, such as a Riesling, but I should think that then the blackcurrant liqueur takes over the taste.

Vin blanc cassis is colloquially known as *un Kir*. The Burgundian has drunk white wine spiked with cassis for many years, but the late Canon Félix Kir, Mayor of Dijon, was such a great personality that his name was adopted for the drink – would that we might all expect such a commemoration. This tiny little man was one of the heroes of the French Resistance in World War II. (On one occasion, when actually the target of a German firing squad, he rose, as if from the dead, and charged at them.) The Beaujolais version of *vin blanc cassis* is made with red wine and the drink is called *rince cochon*, meaning pigswill; however, when the late Nikita Kruschev, President of the USSR, visited the region, it was felt that, when offered to him, the drink could hardly be referred to by such a name, so, for the occasion, the bright red apéritif was renamed *un Nikita*.

A *vin d'honneur* means a drink offered to honour the visitor. If you're lucky it'll be Champagne, but in a wine region it might be the local apéritif. A *vin gris* is a very pale pink wine – the name seems to have been applied particularly to the pale pink wines of Lorraine, but nowadays there are some others which are lilac-toned in colour.

Vin de curé is a French expression for a sharp and virtually undrinkable wine – the sort that somebody very hard up might just manage to afford. But *vinum theologicum* signifies the best wine – the reasoning behind the name seems to be that the saints deserve it, the sinners need it!

Beware of *vin de singe*: this is referred to as the 'wine of ape' in the *Prologue to the Manciple's Tale*, in Chaucer's *Canterbury Tales*. This is because those who drink immoderately of wine become, progressively, meek and quiet as lambs, ferocious and brave as lions, snortingly brutish as pigs and, finally, as maniacal as apes. (Some people may feel this is rather unfair on the ape, but the stages of intoxication are well defined.)

The date when the wine is made can attract a variety of names, especially in Germany, where the vintage, later than in the rest of Europe anyway, may take place in December, or even in the year following that in which it would be expected to occur. My friend Walter Sichel has listed the following: *St Hubertuswein* is a wine made from grapes picked on the 3rd November; *St Martinswein* is made from those that are picked on the 11th November; *St Katharinenwein* from grapes gathered on 25 November; *St Nikolauswein* from grapes gathered on the 6th December and *Christwein* from grapes picked on the 24th or 25th December. Wine made from grapes picked on the Epiphany, 6th January, the day on which the Three Wise Men visited the infant Jesus, is called *Heiliger Dreikönigswein*.

Walter adds notes on wines with names describing what they might be, or might have been, like. *Kometenwein* was made to commemorate the appearance of a comet, the best-known being that of 1811. Some other old vintages from other wine regions may be referred to as 'Comet' wines. *Schwedenwein* was made in the year when the Swedes invaded Europe, at the start of the Thirty Years War (1619–48) under Augustus Adolphus. The description must be disparaging as the Swedes committed terrible atrocities.

Then there are other pejorative expressions. *Strumpfwein* is a wine so sour that it would contract the holes in stockings; one drop of *Fahnenwein* spilt on the regimental colours would shrink

the banner and collect a battalion of soldiers around; *Schulwein* is a sour wine with which parents threaten children unwilling to go to school: 'Only schulwein for supper if you don't get up *now*.' Then there is *Wendewein*, made on the Bodensee, so sour that drinkers have to turn over from time to time in the night, because otherwise the wine will burn a hole in their stomachs while they sleep. In some villages there is even supposed to be a little night bell called the *Wendeglöclein*, rung to remind sleepers to turn over and thereby escape damaging their insides. *Dreimännerwein* is so strong that three men have to drink from a single glass of it so that none of them risks getting drunk, and *Apostelwein* is a stronger version, of which twelve people are required to finish a single glass, so that no one shall suffer unduly from consuming it. (In a similar story told of a Breton wine, two men have to prop the drinker up against a wall, so that he can get the wine down. I had thought this an old tale, but recently saw this wine offered in a London shop – one does hope that, although the name is the same, the wine is not.) *Elefantenwein* refers to wines that were made in both Tübingen and Reutlingen in Württemberg, from grapes so hard it would have required an elephant to crush them.

Well-what *is* in the name?

One of the most hopeful signs concerning British wine drinking – with more than eight litres per head annually swigged, we're nudging the US consumption figure – is that people are no longer shy of at least trying to pronounce wine names.

Of course it does look intimidating when a word is written in olde Germanic scripte and is about two inches long, but nowadays many of us realise that this word may merely mean 'Co-operative' or be the extended noble name of some historic family; since the upper echelons of our landed gentry are spattered with such foreigner-frightening names as Marjoribanks, Ernle-Erle-Drax, Fetherstonhaugh, Cholmondeley and our maps are covered with place names that, spoken, sound totally unlike the way they are spelled (Beaulieu, Leicester, Warwick, Greenwich), we should try to get our tongues around wine names. True, there are some, of which Échezeaux is perhaps the supreme example, that are said never to be 'selling names' because the British won't risk sounding silly when ordering them, but as many of these wines are in minute supply, perhaps this doesn't matter.

Anyway, we no longer seem timid about mispronouncing a foreign word and there is even an advertising campaign urging people to say 'Veeno verdy', when the delightful 'green wine' of north Portugal in fact is pronounced 'Veenyo vaird'. It may be that we shall evolve versions of wine names, as we have done for certain places, such as

Firenze, Lisboa, even Paris, and that the offering of wines as 'Riceling' and 'Chabliss' is almost an affectionate way of referring to them. The only important thing is that, if you *do* say 'Riceling' and 'Chabliss' you get the wine you want – and not either rice wine or, maybe, Chablais, the Swiss wine.

There is certainly a trend to label wines according to the grape that makes them. These names are easy to understand – although the different versions of 'Riesling' that crop up around the world make one long for an international wine board controlling nomenclature: for

A few very rare bottles offered for sale at the auctions of Christie Manson & Woods, in London. Left to right: Tokay Eszencia, of the legendary 'Comet' vintage of 1811 (see page 82); a labelled claret bottle, dating from about 1844; a striking label of the 'Carruades de Mouton', 1927; a sealed bottle of 1874 Lafite, from Brampeth Castle; Prince Metternich's 1870 'Castle Johannisberg', bearing the description 'first growth'; a bottle of 'Crème de thé', a rare tea liqueur from Martinique. This, from about 1830, is the oldest pictorial wine or spirit label known.

example, in Australia, the Hunter River Riesling is actually the Sémillon, the South Australia Riesling is the Crouchen Riesling (no relation at all), which is also the Cape Riesling of South Africa. None of these is the great Rheinriesling – which may also be referred to as White Riesling, Weisse-riesling, or Johannesburg Riesling.

Some drinkers like everything made simple and even suppose wines made wholly or predominantly of one grape variety to be somehow 'better' than those made from several grapes, in dif-

ferent proportions. This works very well – until you ask these purists how they justify the existence of claret!

Indeed, the word 'claret' strikes oddly on the ear of almost everyone except a Briton. Recently there was an attempt to enforce the use of the term 'red Bordeaux' and the mighty EEC thought this was a good idea. The British contingent at Brussels pointed out that, not only had the English crown

owned the Bordeaux region for 299 years (1154–1453), but that, even after being obliged to quit their holding, their purchases of the red wines of Bordeaux had remained substantial and their use of the word 'claret' had continued. The EEC gave in.

During the medieval period, the red wines of Bordeaux were lighter in colour – *plus clair* – than those that came from the hinterland to be shipped through the port of Bordeaux; in fact in very poor years these darker coloured wines might have been used to 'help' the 'plus clair' pale ones. But claret was what red Bordeaux became to the English and the Scots, who were particularly popular in the Gironde – so, consequently, the UK still says 'claret'. Conservatives that we are in temperament, we shall probably continue to do.

The German term for sparkling wine in general is *sekt*. This is another friendly word. In the 19th century, the great German actor, Ludwig Devrient, became famous for his playing of Falstaff. After the theatre, he would call for 'A cup of sack!', in character, when going round to the wine cellar for a refresher – and although he actually required a good beaker of Champagne, a sparkling wine became, in Germany, synonymous with 'sack' – sekt.

The town of Hochheim, on the River Main, is supposed to have given the word 'hock' to the English language and many books will tell you that this is because Queen Victoria and her Albert loved the wines. But *The Shorter Oxford Dictionary* gives the earliest use of the word as 1625; the Jacobeans rendered the name 'Hochheimer' as 'Hockamore'. Though they also referred to 'Rhenish', getting themselves out of the difficulty of awkward foreign names by lumping all German wines together as wines from the Rhine.

A name that really might have been invented by a modern press officer is Est! Est!! Est!!!, which is the wine of Montefiascone, in the Lazio region of Italy. It is white, may be dry, or slightly sweet and even slightly sparkling. It gets its name from the 12th century, when Bishop Johann Fugger, of the famous banking family, whose newsletters give so much information about life at that time, was travelling from his see at Augsburg to Rome, for the coronation of the Emperor Henry V. The Bishop enjoyed the good things of life and prudently sent his steward ahead on the route, so as to ensure suitable fare would be available when he arrived. If the steward approved of the local wine, he was to chalk 'Est!' on the inn door – very much in the way that tramps today mark gates and walls to signify whether or not food and money may be available at the house. When the steward got to

Old-style tasting in an Italian cellar – not, in fact very different from what might be seen today. Some kind of Spanish wine appears to be being drawn from the nearest cask, but a variety of other wines are named on the heads of the casks above. The most important lady visitor has been given the largest glass and provided with cheese and bread to accompany her tasting.

Montefiascone, however, he was so delighted that he chalked three 'Ests!' and stayed on – as did the Bishop, who never reached Rome at all and indeed died where he stopped. His will stipulated that a whole cask of wine should be poured over his grave on each anniversary of his death, but the local bishop didn't approve at all, directing that the wine should be sent to the local seminary, for the enjoyment of the inmates. (One suspects *his* steward may have taken a generous measure for the episcopal household as well.)

The names of owners or firms on wine labels often stand for more than the buyer may suppose and, rather oddly, it is seldom that anyone makes much publicity out of this. Codorníu, the mighty sparkling wine producer, is a name deriving from the Catalan word for quail – a charming and, certainly, gastronomic bird. The three towers on the label of the great firm of TORRES, also in the Penedès region of Spain, are an obvious play on the name, but it is now usually forgotten that, in former times the names of many vineyards were associated with watchtowers: in the Gironde there are seventy-seven estates (as listed in the Bordeaux 'bible', the directory still known as Cocks & Féret – although the 1982 edition is attributed to Féret alone – which gives all the properties) named 'Latour', or 'La Tour', with various suffixes. Château Latour itself, the great first growth of Pauillac, shows on its label the dumpy tower, similar to the Martello towers built around Britian against a possible Napoleonic invasion, which gives a good look out over the river, from which pirates and enemies might attack.

One might have expected another tower at the boundary of St. Estèphe and Pauillac – where the road winds sharply upwards and the Germans in World War II mounted a gun emplacement on the roof of Cos d'Estournel, the odd, Chinese-looking château, where there is no 'château'. For the ornate door, once that of the harem of the Sultan of Zanzibar, opens straight into the *chai*, or above-ground store of wine. Cos d'Estournel and its neighbour, Cos Labory, get their prefixes from the same word – *clos* – as many Burgundy vineyards, where it signifies an enclosed space; in Bordeaux the final 's' is sounded (as in 'cos lettuce'), just as it is in several place names, such as Moulis. Some people think this is because of the 299 years of English occupation. The great St Estèphe estate Montrose, however, has nothing to do with Scotland's hero: it was originally Mont Rose, the pink hill, because, at one time, it seems to have been covered with heather.

Palmer, at Margaux, likewise had nothing to do with either holy pilgrims or the biscuit dynasty, but takes its name from Sir Charles Palmer, a great personality of the Regency period, who had

above right *The label of the 1975 Château Mouton-Rothschild, designed by Andy Warhol. Baron Philippe de Rothschild has asked a number of world-famous artists to design the great wine's labels and displays of them attract many viewers at exhibitions.*

below right *The card of a representative of Julius Kayser of Traben – the lady seems to be drinking a glass of sekt (see page 86).*

Dessin inédit   *Andy Warhol*

1975
cette récolte à produit
247.000 bouteilles bordelaises et demies
9.223 magnums, jéroboams, impériales

Philippe de Rothschild

Château
Mouton Rothschild

LE BARON PHILIPPE PROPRIETAIRE
APPELLATION PAUILLAC CONTRÔLÉE

75cl

PRODUCE OF FRANCE

TOUTE LA RECOLTE MISE EN BOUTEILLES AU CHATEAU

come to know and like the Bordeaux region when spending some leave there, after taking part in Wellington's campaign in the Iberian Peninsula. He was a very rich man and bought the property from a young widow with whom he found himself journeying overnight in a coach to Paris, where she was going to dispose of the estate. Palmer unfortunately went bankrupt, being very unwise in all money matters, and also because the Prince Regent disdained this fine, delicate claret in favour of a much commercialised brew in vogue at that time in chic London. Subsequently, the Palmer estate was bought by the banking family of Pereire, whose initials and not Sir Charles' are the 'Ps' in the decorations on the château they built. Palmer, like Montrose, is one of those estates on which the pronunciation varies, according to which language you're speaking: 'Palmer' as in 'Huntley and' and Montrose; or, in French, 'Pallmaire', and 'Monrose', with no sounding of the middle 't'. The latter ruling also applies to the great Burgundy vineyard, Le Montrachet, for this name originates in the Latin *mons rachicensis* – the hill from which the trees have been uprooted – and no intrusive 't' is voiced.

Carving of vintage scene, from La Trinité, *the abbey church of* Vendôme.

Burgundy vineyard names often started by being descriptive of the soil and aspects of the ground: the site name *Les Cras* apparently can be related in quite direct ways to Welsh, Irish and Breton – and the English word 'crag', meaning a rocky hillock. The Pommard vineyard, Les Rugiens, may indicate the reddish colour of the soil, which apparently contains some ironstone. Sites where spiny bushes and thorny vegetation grew in profusion have caused some vineyards

above left *Rather old-fashioned sherry vintage in the Jerez vineyards in Andalucia, southern Spain.*

below left *Young and old picking grapes at Fleurie in the Beaujolais – whose jovial inhabitants tend to have ample curves similar to those of the local bottles.*

to be called *Épenots* and *Épenotts* and at Chambolle-Musigny the *Les Groseilles* plot has survived centuries after the gooseberries (*groseilles*) have ceased to be planted there. (According to the scholarly work by Marie-Hélène Landrieu-Lussigny, *Les vignobles bourguignons, ses lieux-dits*', Jeanne Laffitte, Marseille 1983.)

Names often indicate the fact that much vineyard ground is poor and useless for anything except vines: *Les Vaucrains* at Nuits St Georges and the name *Comblanchien* both seem once to have signified *Les vaut rien* – good for nothing. The vineyards around Don Quixote's country of La Mancha in southern Spain take their name, *Valdepeñas*, from 'Valley of Stones'. But Nierstein, in the Rheinhessen district of Germany, is so called because the Latin *neri* and *stein* here meant the boundary stone between the two regions, one of which formerly belonged to the Germans and the other to the Franks. This is somewhat more picturesque than the *Gerumpel* vineyard at Wachenheim, which signifies 'rubbish dump'; the place may once have been the local tip. The Marcobrunn vineyard in the Rheingau is named for the spring (*brunnen*) dedicated to St Mark, which divides Erbach and Hattenheim; at one time both villages claimed ownership of the spring, but eventually it was decided that it belonged to Erbach. The following night, some wit from Hattenheim wrote on the wall enclosing the spring 'Erbach has the water – but Hattenheim has the wine'.

One of the most famous of all German vineyards is on the Mosel – the Sonnenuhr or sundial site, where a chunk of the vineyard has been sliced away and painted so that there is actually a large white sundial in the middle of vines. A little up the same river is the Doktor site at Bernkastel, which is said to have got its name in the 14th century, when Archbishop Bohemund II, then Elector of Trier, became ill while staying at Landshut Castle, the ruin which towers so picturesquely over the twin towns of Bernkastel and Kues. He is said to have made a miraculous recovery after drinking some of the local wine – stroke of good fortune for the vineyard.

Then there are the names that seem a bit jokey: Pepys' 'Ho Bryan', (Haut Brion) really cannot be related to the Emerald Isle – another example of an anglicisation of a supposed 'difficult'

A German vintage scene of some years ago –
oxen were used in many vineyards, and,
although slow-moving, they could accomplish
a great deal of work, although they had to be
muzzled so as not to nibble the grapes.

right   A new vineyard is started – and
various 'baptismal gifts' are hung on a nearby
tree to convey good wishes and luck.

left   Typical sundial dominating a vineyard in
the Mosel. The walls restrain the soil from
slipping down the very steep slopes. Probably
the notion of putting sundials in vineyards
originated in the time when workers might be
out of sight or sound of a church or public
clock to tell them the time.

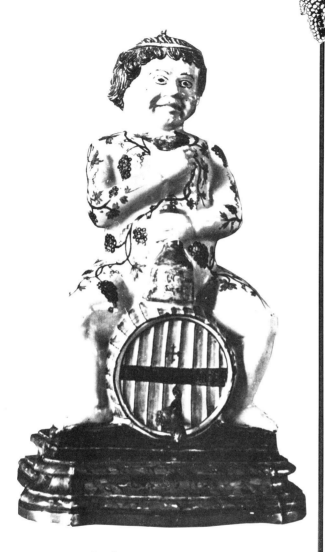

wine name — but the popular Lynch-Bages estate certainly can, because it once belonged to a Monsieur Lynch, who was an Irishman and mayor of Bordeaux. The deep brown Greek wine, Mavrodaphne, is supposed to get its name from a beautiful, dark-haired nymph (*mavro* signifies dark), but I have a feeling that there must be something more to naming a particularly luscious wine than just giving it the name of a girlfriend; the 'Daphne' part of the name is a bit unfortunate, because she was the nymph who, pursued against her will by Apollo, shrieked for help and was obligingly turned into a laurel bush. One imagines the god, balked of his prey, seizing on some toiling peasant nearby and saying, 'Give me a drink!', rewarding the man with the promise that his vines should bear particularly good fruit — 'And that, my girl,' one can hear him saying to the quivering laurel bush 'will teach you to run away when we might have had such a nice little get-together'. If he had then turned her into a vine it might have been friendlier.

How the Yugoslav Radgonda Ranina got its name — which means 'Tiger Milk' — no one has explained either. Was some local hero suckled by a tiger to whom he thereafter attributed his feats of arms? Or is it like the Hungarian Bull's Blood of Eger — Egri Bikavér — which was the 'quick lift' with which the women of Eger refreshed those defending the city against the Turks in 1552; not being in a situation that encouraged refined eating or drinking at the time, the hirsute warriors tossed off huge amounts of the red wine, thereby staining their beards. The teetotal Mohammedan besiegers, unable to understand the continuing valour of the Hungar-

Bacchus sitting on a cask — in fact, the whole is an antique bottle, from La Mission Haut Brion in the Graves region of Bordeaux.

right *Ancient brandy bottles, the labels of some obviously intended to appeal to the customers likely to be attracted by the Napoleonic references. The 1904 Grande Fine Champagne is in a 15th century bottle.*

ians, assumed that their courage and the red that dyed their beards must have come from the blood of that bravest of beasts, the bull. I'm told that the name is disliked by some of the British public as 'nasty', but what can be repellent about it I can't understand; in these days we're wise enough to pump blood *into* people rather than draining it out of them, as in the comparatively recent days of leechcraft, so one would suppose it to be a Good Thing and any beverage associated with it heroic and benevolent.

du Pape, which got its name when the Pope had his headquarters – and a sizable portion of vineyard – at Avignon instead of in Rome. For this reason, some of the bottles used for the wines bear the crossed keys of St Peter's successor. But Beaumes de Venise, well-known for its sweet wine, is so called because, in Provençal, the first word meant 'grotto' and the second, *venaissin*, signifying a particular fiefdom or plot let out to somebody.

A cheerful name is that of the Rhône vineyard, Gigondas, for it comes from the Latin *jocunditas* – the merry city. This is less pompous than Châteauneuf

The Sardinian wine, named Anghelu Ruju, one feels, really must have a story to it, for it means 'Red Angel'. As it's above table wine strength, its action

might be more that of a red devil, if drunk with a meal. Likewise, the Spanish word *lágrima*, meaning tear, may suggest a romantic tale is attached thereto – but in fact the truth is more prosaic: when this wine of Málaga is made in the traditional way, only the free-flowing juice from the grapes being used, the liquid drops slowly, tear-like, from the press. While the word 'tears' (the kind you weep) is used widely in Spain for the trails that slide slowly down the sides of the glass after the wine has been swirled around, isn't it somehow indicative of national character that whereas the French term these trails 'legs', the Germans call them 'Gothic windows'?

The Germans, whom one might have expected to be exact about wine names, in view of their immensely complicated German Wine Law, confuse the foreigner with the pink wine that, in Baden-Württemberg, is referred to as 'Schillerwein'. In fact the word comes, not from the poet's name, but from the German for 'shimmer' or 'glitter'; still, I have seen references to 'Schillerwein' being the poet's 'favourite tipple' by writers who didn't verify the reference. (Having once got the Rheingau and the Rheinhessen the wrong way round when I was being hustled by an editor, I do know how these things can happen.)

Which cues me in to the curious names borne by some grapes as well as wines. Blanquette de Limoux gets its name from the white underside of the leaves of the Mauzac grape from which it is wholly or partly made. Harslevelü, a Hungarian white grape, is so called because the leaf shape is similar to that of the lime flower – which is the translation of the Hungarian word. The Pinot Meunier grape, used in Champagne, is a black grape with an intense white down on its leaves, like the powdering of flour of a miller's coat, *meunier* being French for miller. And the Blanc Fumé grape, used in the upper reaches of the River Loire (and, to my mind, idiotically transposed as Fumé Blanc in some New World vineyards) is merely the local name for the Sauvignon. It's worth stressing this because, many years ago, the aberration of a friend started a new legend.

The friend was lecturing to a group in the north of England, which included several Masters of Wine (before whom all knees bow!) in the front row. He was asked the meaning of the term *blanc fumé*. I may say that many of the Loire grapes have nicknames, but I've not yet discovered the origin of this one. The lecturer hadn't the experience to say he didn't know, or that he did know but had forgotten; unwisely, he decided he must say *something*. So – he announced that in that part of the Loire, the vineyards were much troubled by 'morning wind'. The expression on the faces of the Masters of Wine nearly made him choke at this point but he went on. This morning wind, said he, blew the bloom off the grapes, which then settled in a white mist – *blanc fumé* – above the vineyards. . . . And this little bit of wine lore continues to turn up in features by writers who, unfortunately, have not been able to find out anything else. I wish they would – and tell me.

The grape sometimes referred to as *bon breton* in the middle Loire is the Cabernet Franc, named after Richelieu's intendant, the Abbé Breton. When the town that bears the great Cardinal's name was being laid out, the Abbé was sent down to Bordeaux to bring back cuttings for the vineyards and it was the Cabernet Franc vine that yielded best. There are those who aver that there was an established earlier market for the red Loire wines with the Bretons – I admit I don't see this as being more than slightly possible. Why the Pineau de la Loire (the Chenin Blanc) got its nickname I don't know. But it shouldn't be confused with *pinard*, which is the wine ration served to Frenchmen doing their national service.

The word 'Tent', which is sometimes seen on old wine labels, is thought by some people to be an anglicised version of *tinta* – red. Others associate it with wines of south-west Spain, such as Alicante and Málaga. 'Mountain', another wine label word, seems also to be associated with Málaga.

Ancient bottles of Château Lafite Rothschild, in the cellars of the Eiffel Tower restaurant in Paris. The label of the 1846 looks surprisingly 'young' and in fact, in earlier times the name was spelled 'Lafitte' but, as the Rothschilds have never altered the label's design, the paper may have been of a later date. Note the pepperpot tower, although it's not easy to see the five arrows transfixing it – they signify the five Rothschild brothers who started the great business houses in various different countries.

Those who admire the great Mouton-Rothschild, may not realise that the old French word for 'mound' is associated with it – quite rightly, because it's the hillocks or *croupes* that can make all the difference between one segment of vineyard and its neighbour. *Motte* is a place and family name and Bordeaux dialect apparently used to render it as *Mothon* – hence *Mouton*, in this case nothing to do with sheep, although the notion of pasture is pleasant. The representations of sheep on the labels of the property, which the owner, Baron Philippe, commissions from different artists, and the impressive ram's head snuff holder in the wonderful museum at the château are agreeable visual puns, but possibly no more than that. Anyway, the word for hillock or mound in Old French is *fite*, – hence Lafite-Rothschild. The lesser known Arsac fifth growth, Le Tertre, apparently means the same sort of thing.

Family names are of course often incorporated in estate names. The ancient property named Calon-Ségur came into the hands of the Ségur family in the 18th century; the then head of the family, known as *le Prince des Vignes* is credited with the saying, 'I make my wine at Lafite and Latour, but my heart is at Calon' and this is why the Calon-Ségur label bears a heart to this day. The origin of the word *Calon* is obscure, although Clive Coates (in *Claret*, Century 1982) points out, somewhat frivolously, that *Calon* is Welsh for 'heart' and *Segur* is Welsh for 'safe'! More reliably, it may be said that *Calon* is an old word for 'wood', and that the local name for the shallow boats that took wood across the Gironde estuary was *calons* or *chalonnes*. But one thinks wonderingly of anyone who owned Lafite, Latour and Calon. . . .

Another pleasant tale is associated with Château Margaux, where the quartz content of the soil caused a past owner, the Comte d'Hargicourt, godson of Madame Dubarry, to appear at the court of Louis XV wearing enormous lustrous buttons on his coat (or waistcoat). When asked what these stones were by the King – then obviously getting on a bit – and hard up after various wars – the Comte replied, 'They are the diamonds of my estate.' The fact that this story is also told about Château Latour does not make it less credible – it only illustrates that the nobility of the period bothered more about what they wore than about the wines made on their properties.

The famous dessert wine of Cyprus, Commandaria, gets its name from early medieval times, when the island was divided into *commanderies*, or sections; it was the Knights of Saint John of Jerusalem – the 'Knights of the White Cross' – famous for their heroic exploits against the Turks, who had charge of the particular commanderie where the best wine was made. I am tempted to comment that, as the Knights of St John were rigidly debarred from most worldly pleasures, the making of wine did at least enable them to enjoy one of the good things of life.

Then there are the territorial names. Aquitania, the old name for the huge duchy forming the south-west of France, comes from the Latin phrase, meaning 'land of waters'; Entre-Deux-Mers signifies the region 'between two seas' – in other words, between the rivers Dordogne and Garonne. Graves is a name obviously referring to the type of soil (gravel), but Médoc may be a contraction of the Latin *in medio acquae* – in the middle of the waters; in other words, between the Atlantic and the Gironde estuary.

The gardens of Château Beychevelle, in St. Julien in the Médoc, are particularly beautiful.

There are semi-political names. Beychevelle got its name for fiscal reasons. It was originally called the Château de Médoc at Lamarque, where there are still ruins of fortifications and imposing seignorial buildings looking along the estuary. In 1587 the heiress of the Château de Médoc married the Duc d'Épernon, Grand Admiral of France and the estate went with her. This duke seems to have been a somewhat dreary person, his wastrel descendants making it no wonder the family died out in 1666. But the Grand Admiral, a favourite of the effeminate Henri III, is said to have insisted on ships going up and down the Gironde striking their sails in salute as they passed his property, the expression *beche velle* being Gascon for *baissez les voiles* – strike sails – whereupon the château became Beychevelle. There are those who affirm that the Duc d'Épernon never lived at Beychevelle (did his wife though, one wonders, just so as to be apart from him?), but what does seem to be a matter of history is that on one of the islands in the estuary, opposite the estate, there was a cypress tree, a type of foliage that is always noticeable, especially when growing in the middle of a wide river, and it was this point at which outgoing vessels had to stop and pay dues to local authorities; this would certainly have involved them striking their sails. Anyway, this is the background to the ship on the Beychevelle label. The Grand Admiral may have resided in his huge and ornate château at Cadillac, which is now the headquarters of the local white wine fraternity, after having served as a women's prison for some years.

There does not seem to have ever been any definite connection between the Earl of Shrewsbury, Shakespeare's 'brave Talbot', who was killed at the Battle of Castillon in 1453 and the St Julien estate, Château Talbot; and, as the name is invariably pronounced French-wise, the final 't' being silent, maybe the English association is not founded on fact. Château Ausone, the great St Émilion property, is traditionally associated with the poet Ausonius, who, in the 4th century, is said to have lived on the site at his Villa Lucania; but as there are several other sites suggested for the villa, Ausonius' country house is to the Gironde what the beds in which Queen Elizabeth I slept are to various places in England.

In some New World wine regions very old words are also in use to name the wines or the estates. For example, the Napa Valley is possibly the best-known California wine area and my colleague, Cyril Ray, always meticulous in his research, explains in *Robert Mondavi of the Napa Valley* (Heinemann 1984) that the word Napa – often misspelled by the British as 'Nappa', with leathery associations – may have come from the Indian Wappo tribe. Some people, says Cyril, think that this was the Indian word for 'homeland' or, alternatively, 'fish'; but, he adds, 'Many believe that this was not an Indian word at all . . . but a corruption of the Spanish 'guapo', brave . . . yet one more guess, for none is more than a guess, is that it was the Indian word for 'plenty'.'

Yet few California wine names seem very imaginative. There is Beaulieu, pronounced in California as 'Bowlyou', always a stumbling block for the Briton, accustomed to 'Bewley', which is now apparently abbreviated to 'B.L.' in the interests of sales to those who can't cope with a supposedly awkward French word. The word, of course, merely means a beautiful place.

The Hanzell Winery of Sonoma gets its name because the owner, James D. Zellabach, combined his name with that of his wife, Hana; the winery is said to be laid out on the lines of Clos de Vougeot, although Mr. Zellabach had been US Ambassador to Italy, not France. Buena Vista, the original vineyard of an amaz-

ing Hungarian, Agostón Harászthy, means 'beautiful view'. And, says Leon M. Adams, the authority on American wines, the stag of the famous 'Stag's Leap' property is a legendary beast. Otherwise, vineyards here mainly seem to take the name of the original owner, even if the present proprietor is in no way associated with the German,

California vintage scene, around 1880. The treaders are standing on lattices of wood, through which the crushed grapes will drop down to the huge vats. On the left a press is being operated, either to squeeze the last drops of juice out of the mush of debris left by the treaders, or for pressing poorer quality grapes, the juice from which may go to the distillery. On the right, some of the must is being examined.

French, Spanish or Italian wine growers who laid down the vineyards.

The same tends to be true of the names of many of the vineyards in Australia and New Zealand, where there are many wine dynasties still active – sometimes, rather confusingly, working for firms bearing other names. A big book remains to be written about these families and their traditions, which would be quite as fascinating as any history of Bordeaux or the port shippers. There are also some charming names that make use of aboriginal words. Coonawarra, that curious flat South Australian region that contradicts all the otherwise established theories that wine of fine quality can only be made from vines grown on a slope, means 'wild honeysuckle'; Yalumba, widely-known and also in South Australia, means 'all the country round'; the historic estate, Château Tahbilk in the Goulburn Valley, north of Melbourne, gets its name from 'tabilk tabilk' which, says authority Len Evans, means in aboriginal, 'place of many watering holes' – how the 'h' got into the name, when the nearby township is definitely Tabilk, no one knows.

At Château Tahbilk, in Victoria, Australia, some of the 1860 original vines, ungrafted prior to the phylloxera plague, are still yielding. The roses at the end of each row of vines are a Bordeaux tradition, both to mark out the different plots and rows and making it difficult for anyone using horses for cultivation to cut corners. But, most important, roses attract pests and show their presence more immediately than vines, so these act rather like the canaries miners used to take down the mines to check on the air supply – they are early-warning devices.

In Canada, Argentina and Chile also, wines tend to get their names from those of wine families, firms or the nearest town. It's rather sad that, with English wines developing so interestingly, their names incline to be somewhat plain and vaguely evocative of the local associations. There's Beaulieu, whose vineyard is thought by some to be haunted by the ghosts of the monks who ran the vineyard for the great abbey before the dissolution of the monasteries; Three Choirs, associated with the famous festival and Hambledon, where the first cricket match was played, are two slightly more exciting place names. Although it might be difficult for supermarket shoppers to grasp the significance of any Anglo-Saxon or even Middle English name (what about 'Beowulf's Beaker', or 'Sir Gawaine'?), I see no reason why 'A Canterbury Tale', 'Danegeld' (for an East Anglian wine), or, certainly 'Battle' for something of Hastings provenance, should fail to attract. The local wine, served to Her Majesty Queen Elizabeth II on a recent visit to Jersey – 'Your Queen, our Duke' as the Jersey people say – was from La Mare vineyard, the name meaning 'the sea'. (The owner has put a signpost in the middle of his vineyard, showing just how many miles it is to all the great classic vineyards of the world.)

At the Cape in South Africa, however, the advantage of many different languages being employed in everyday life, plus the richness contributed by the different settlers who have developed the wine business since the 17th century, are obvious. Many people will not know that Afrikaans itself, developed as a result of the blend of local languages and the speech of the French, Dutch, British and German farmers, was not an official language at all until very recently. The Afrikaans names of many of the great wine estates have been given to them in affection, almost as 'little names' are bestowed within a family and relate to their appearance, the view from them, associations with European origins, or local expressions.

Tasting in a Canadian winery – good wines are now being made here.

Vintaging in Stellenbosch, South Africa. Note the typical Cape Dutch architecture with the curved gables and, in the background, the mountains which, ever changing in colour, have won the sobriquet 'fairest vineyards' for this beautiful wine region.

There is beautiful Meerlust, which means 'sea view' – my friend Graham Knox in his book on the Cape estates explains that there is only one farm between Meerlust and the sea and that the property's humid conditions are similar to those prevailing in many of the Bordeaux estates. There is Uiterwyk, which means 'outer ward', derived from the grazing around the Dutch village of Kampen; today, in Holland, Uiterwyk is a suburb of Kampen. The Briton is told to pronounce Uitkyk as 'ate cake' and this estate, with its enchanting house, supposed to have been built according to plans filched from the architect Thibault, who had designed it for a house in Cape Town, means 'outlook'. Most moving of all, is Allesverloren, in the Swartland; the property, under vines since the early 18th century, was the birthplace of a former Prime Minister of South Africa, D.F. Malan, one of whose family still owns it.

But Allesverloren got its name in the late 18th century; the then owners used to go to Stellenbosch to attend church every three weeks; during one of their absences, the journey taking many hours, the local Bushmen came and raided the farm, burning the buildings and dispersing the stock. On their return, the churchgoers stared down from the mountain pass at what was a complete ruin and one of them commented, 'All is lost' – Allesverloren. It's a tribute to the farmers that they rebuilt, rehabilitated and re-established the estate, which today is one of the most respected of the region. A happier name is that of the Breede River estate, Weltevrede, which means 'well satisfied' – as drinkers of their wines today are sure to be.

The Tulbagh property, Twee Jongegezellen, now often gets its name abbreviated to 'T.J.', although actually it's not very difficult to pronounce. (The real tongue twister, which friends tease me into attempting, is Overgaauw, because the guttural in the middle of the word is alien to a *roineck* – or 'redneck', the Afrikaans nickname for a Briton in the Boer War, because the fair-skinned soldiers caught the sun so unfortunately.) The 'two friends' who joined forces and farmed the T.J. property in the 17th century, were bachelors, although they needn't have been 'good friends' in the sense that our permissive society might suppose. Their names are lost to us, like those of the two young men in the wine trade, who, travelling for their firm in 1678, found a particularly good wine in the monastery at Lamego, ideal for shipping to the British market; the abbot explained that he had added brandy to the cask, during fermentation . . . thus port as we know it came into being.

Champagne and its niceties

It's one of the infuriating things about gastronomic and wine history that often the conventions of a period are so much taken for granted by those observing them that they are never written down. People are supposed to know about these matters if they are in a particular social category, those who are not are not interested.

For example, the memoirs of Leonard Russell, give an account of how Russell, at the age of sixteen, was obliged to play host in an otherwise feminine household to the great Mr Gladstone; young Russell remained at the table with the statesman after the ladies had retired and records, tantalizingly, that when the decanter was produced, Gladstone said, as if talking to himself, 'This is very good port they have given me – but why do they serve it in a claret glass?' What did he mean? True, port glasses can be smaller than those usually provided for claret – but not that much. Was the glass different in shape? Was it a cut glass, or did it possess some attribute of the glass commonly used at the time for claret? Russell and Gladstone were fully conversant with good food and wine, indeed, interested in both and their well-to-do-households certainly had well-stocked cellars. Russell remembered the event. But he does not explain it.

The first mystery I encountered in relation to Champagne was as the guest of an eminent shipper, then agent for Pol Roger. His London luncheon room had, on the sideboard, an object that consisted of a bulbous flask or carafe, unable to stand, reclining on its side in a rectangular glass vessel, which was rather like a shoebox with a slot cut out at one end, in which the neck of the carafe or decanter could rest. It was suggested that this appliance would have been used as a container or cooler for the still wine of Champagne – but the host was firm that, at the period from which it was possible to date the device, no still wine was made by that particular Champagne establishment. Surely no one would have wished to decant Champagne, thereby depriving it of much, if not all of its effervescence? Yet the name of the Champagne house, Pol Roger, was engraved on the flask. What purpose did this vessel serve?

For years I asked everyone who might know but no one could provide an answer. Then one day, talking with a friend interested in wine, but handling the public relations for a big French establishment making top quality kitchen utensils, I happened to mention this strange and puzzling appliance. She told me that, on a recent visit to the mighty manufacturer, she had remained talking with the host in the room in which luncheon was to be served while the group, of which someone else was in charge, was taken around the works. To her surprise, he produced several carafes and proceeded to open and decant several bottles of Champagne into them. On her asking why he did this the reply was immediate.

'But you *must* have Champagne decanted if you're going to drink it at luncheon!' Apparently they always decanted it and always had done.

The implication is that a wholly fizzy wine, served throughout a meal, may be somewhat too gassy for the ordinary digestion to cope with comfortably. The late Raymond Postgate (1896–1971) a dear friend of mine, once wrote in his almost 18th century style about a meal at which Champagne had been served at every course and recorded his resulting

above right *From 'Le Rire', an artist's idea as to how people in the provinces suppose the Parisians celebrate Reveillon.*

below right *Relief of Dom Pierre Pérignon in the cloisters of the Abbey of Hautvillers in Champagne, where he became cellarmaster.*

discomfort; for, as he said, the only way to get rid of a lot of gas in the stomach is to belch – and when you are young and shy, you don't deliberately belch in public. So one mystery seems to have been solved.

Further enlightenment on bubbles was provided on an occasion when I was giving a lecture on Champagne, and somebody asked a question about the swizzle stick. This is a loathsome object, which, produced in gold and silver by chic boutiques for the person who has everything, or presented in nightclubs as wooden sticks resembling porridge spirtles, covered in twirls of coloured tissue, is rightly condemned by any lover of the world's supreme sparkling wine. All the trouble and time that has gone into retaining the sparkle for which you're paying, is set at nought if you then take the sparkle out; sometimes people even whisk a fork in their glass to flatten the bubbly. Why order a fully sparkling wine if this is not going to agree with you, when there are probably plenty of acceptable still wines on the wine list?

My audience and I were exchanging views on this matter when a fascinating contribution was made to the discussion. A member of the audience had been brought up in the Far East, where his father and grandfather had transacted business for many years. His father, he said, had a large collection of swizzle sticks, made from bone, wood of various kinds and precious metals, which were carved, decorated and ornamented in various ways. But, he was firm, he had never seen them used for taking the bubbles out of any sparklng wine.

Before it was possible to purify the water supply of a region, or when people went 'up country', the water that they drank would come from a bottle, for safety's sake. Whether or not this bottled water was always of the fizzy type, I do not know, but certainly it seems mostly to have been so. Bearing this in mind, his suggestion was that those who wanted still water to dilute their brandy or Scotch, took the fizz out of the drink by whisking it with a swizzle stick. It's easy to imagine that, on retirement and back home in Britain, they might have continued to do exactly the same, happily reminiscent, while imbibing their 'sundowner'.

It is not hard to imagine that, in some smart restaurants, clubs or private houses where fashionable people gathered, the person who took out a swizzle stick and whisked his drink attracted attention. The Edwardian age, that of the Belle Époque, went in for all kinds of gadgets for the dining-table and anyone with a shrewd eye to the potential market might have encouraged a jeweller to make up special swizzle sticks to take the bubbles out of drinks. I have never seen a swizzle stick made by Fabergé, but it's the sort of gimmickry beloved in this period.

above left *A Political Dinner, 1821, whereat some participants abuse their constitutions.*

below left *A Snug Cabin, by Rowlandson 1808. (See page 136.)*

When it is remembered that, at this time many men, especially officers in smart regiments, wore corsets to enhance their appearance (friends who have managed to get into some of the dress uniforms of the time assure me that these were a very tight fit indeed), it will be realised that a large consumption of sparkling wine, when one's middle was severely compressed, would result in discomfort – and possible explosions, above or below. The adroit maître d'hôtel, discreetly sliding a swizzle stick alongside the bottle of Champagne, with a mutter that this would make it so much easier to drink, had an eye to increased wine consumption. The wasp-waisted military type, also the 'fine figure of a woman' with her whaleboned 'Grecian bend' curves, would appreciate a slightly less gassy drink. I do not think that many wines were then made of the pétillant, or slightly sparkling, type. It was a fully gasified wine or nothing – don't forget that a huge quantity of Champagne was then being made, some of which may not have been wholly good or easily digestible.

It is a pity that a harmless device, making drinks palatable in sometimes difficult conditions, should have been adapted to the abuse of Champagne. Nowadays we have table waters still or fizzy, as we wish – and does anyone wear corsets except as some sort of titillating sexual accessory?

One spectacular version of serving Champagne is known as 'the cascade'. For this, tiers of glasses are arranged, the bottom row being in a wide circle, succeeding tiers having the bases of the glasses balanced between the bowls of the row underneath. These tiers rise several rows in height, being finally topped by a bottle or a magnum of Champagne, poised on the few glasses in the circle at the top.

Then some gallant Champenois, maybe the head of a particular establishment, possibly formerly trained in the famous Cadre Noir at Saumur (see page 173) approaches the circular pile of glasses and, with one slash of his sabre, knocks the top off the bottle without upsetting the bottle or the glasses, so that the wine foams out and trickles down, filling each tier of glasses in turn, like a wonderful waterfall.

I have never actually seen this dramatic feat performed, though the 'cascade' is a magnificent sight on film. For obvious reasons, it is not attempted every day and one wonders in a prosaic way how people practise in advance – and whether they use the 'real thing' as regards the wine in doing so. I can find no one to tell me whether or not the neck of the bottle is scored in advance; this would seem a prudent measure, if the crack were to be quick and clean.

One problem arose, however, when a shot of this exploit was planned to be shown as part of an advertising campaign for a great Champagne. The authorities who now control advertising standards feared that, if the whole pro-

At the Ritz Casino in London, Baron de Montesquieu, international director of Moët-Hennessy, performs a 'sabrage', knocking the top off the bottle, so that the Champagne foams down the pyramid of glasses.

cess, including the actual moment when the blade struck the neck of the bottle, were to be shown on television, adventurous children might be spurred into trying to imitate the action! So the film was cut to go out showing the sabre flashing through the air, then the Champagne flowing down into the glasses – without the instant of impact.

It is not only possible but not difficult – because I've done it myself – to take the neck off a bottle of port in a somewhat similar way to that in the 'cascade' procedure, but without the cascade effect. The capsule is removed, the neck of the bottle and the top of the cork are wiped clean and the corkscrew inserted to the length of the cork. Then, while the bottle is held steady upright, the flange at the top of the neck is struck smartly from below on both sides with an upward blow from something heavy, such as the back of a big carving knife. This will, literally, crack the bottle, (indicating the origin of the expression) which, I'm sure was done frequently by our ancestors who might not always have had a corkscrew with them. The top, with the cork in it, can then be taken cleanly away by picking up the corkscrew handle and breaking off the bottle's top. I was taught to do this with an empty bottle that had been re-corked and it was surprisingly easy, but it is fair to say that this might well have been an old bottle, with the 'ring' or neck flange having a weaker join than would exist in the modern mass-produced port bottle.

To crack a bottle by using port tongs – which in recent times have been re-manufactured to satisfy the requirements of customers who enjoy buying accessories to the service of wine – the corkscrew is inserted as before. The tongs are heated over a flame. Then a small strip of thin wadding or cloth, soaked in cold water, is tied around the point of the bottle neck where the tongs are to be applied, so that, when they make contact with it, the glass underneath will crack cleanly. It is also possible to crack the glass by applying the tongs first and then wiping the place with a strip of cloth soaked in cold water. Of course, the wine must be decanted from the broken bottle.

There are various general, although not particularised, references to the drinking of Champagne from the slippers of ladies who usually seem to have been stars of the theatre or musical comedy. One of these, Ruby Miller, does mention the gesture in her memoirs. She also says that the admirer involved, one of the Edwardian 'Stage Door Johnnies', of the Gaiety Theatre in the Strand, had several dozen pairs of slippers sent round to her the next day, by way of replacement. It seems a somewhat unsatisfactory way of drinking and of having your shoe employed, although I suppose that, in the excitement of such an occasion, the sogginess of the shoe when put on again went unnoticed.

References to the grandes cocottes who actually bathed in Champagne are also to be found. This type of extravagant gesture is on a par with that of throwing pearls into wine and then drinking the dissolved result, in which the ancient Romans were supposed to indulge.

Regimen sanitatis

Dis ist ein Regiment der gesuntheit durch
alle Monadt des gantzen Jares/wie
man sich halte sol mit essen vnd
auch mit trincken vñ saget
auch von aderlassen.

A fairly recent example of this kind of indulgence occurred when a London wine merchant received successive orders for a 1921 German wine of supreme quality – and astronomic price. The wine came from one of the greatest vintages and those fortunate enough to be able to try it would have done so in appreciative sips. Finally, the supply was exhausted. The order came in again, from the official responsible for ordering on behalf of his master, a maharaja or sultan of fabulous wealth. The wine merchant explained there was no more –

A medieval queen, following a 'régime' involving bathing in wine, watched by a possibly anxious doctor and having a top-up from a servant – was she feeling chilly?

would another wine, slightly less costly, but equally fine, be acceptable? It would certainly provide a final 'high note' on which to end a dinner.

'Oh what a pity,' commented the customer. 'His Highness does like to have a drink last thing at night – he finds this particular wine so refreshing when it's mixed with soda water.'

The area producing Champagne before 1914 was very much larger than it is now and, one suspects, at least some of the wine might not have been up to the standards required by those who drank it, but there is an absence of specific references to bathing in it. Ladies have more commonly publicised bathing in milk – Ziegfield star Anna Held, who actually had baths with starch in the water (to stiffen what? one cannot help wondering) had a churn delivered daily to the Netherlands Hotel in New York, in which she bathed. Some beauties of classical times, like Cleopatra, favoured asses' milk as a personal dip.

Milk must have made the bather very sticky – and the soap would have been hard to find. And if the milk were heated and frothed up, was there a risk of it curdling? Bathing is an agreeable activity – finding oneself surrounded by curds and whey may not be wholly pleasant. Although Warner Allen, (1881–1968) as a very young man, remembered seeing in a shop window in Paris, 'Champagne pour le bain', he admitted that he had never known anyone actually make use of this. I have a slight suspicion that, even if it did contain some form of wine, such bath Champagne was more in the nature of a bath essence, glamorously presented and named before the days of strict controls of nomenclature.

Mid-18th century bottle of Champagne.

left *Champagne songs and dances were popular in the Belle Époque – this, one of the most successful, was to be heard in the music halls throughout Britain.*

There is, of course, the famous bath scene in Harold Robbins' *The Carpet Baggers*, in which the 'heroine' puts her lover in a bath, pours Champagne over him (although, as several of my friends in the Champagne trade have pointed out, this would probably have been New York State 'Champagne' and not the real thing) and then takes a cut-throat razor to shave him all over. What this is supposed to achieve I have never been able to understand. It must have taken some time anyway. And suppose she, as well as her hand, slipped? It all seems a straining after an effect in a peculiarly drawn out, complicated way. Although I have consulted with a number of gentlemen whose worldly experiences might have given them the ability to enlighten me as to the appeal, effect or general attraction of this experience, all have

The Boizel cellars under Épernay, with plenty of mould in evidence. This form of fungus is sometimes referred to as 'the cellarmaster's flower'. It is a benign growth on walls and ceilings and is never cleaned off.

admitted their inability to do so.

A more satisfactory result might have been achieved, I think, had the persons concerned sat down in a social and civilised way and shared a bottle – even a magnum – of the world's supreme sparkler. Even if the 'moving of the earth' or any of those supposedly satisfactory experiences which certain writers attempt to tag on to the sexual act when it appears to be totally distinct from making love, do not come to pass, then at least the parties will have enjoyed a decent drink and may pass into a peaceful sleep. (They can start sharing razors and scrubbing each other's backs when they wake up.)

In the Pommery cellars in the 19th century. The bottles are going up to the surface in their baskets to have the second corks inserted after the process of disgorging.

However, there is one story about a bath in Champagne that has the ring of veracity. Some years ago an eminent London wine shipper, whose portfolio of agencies included a superb Champagne, married a very beautiful woman. During the engagement she mentioned that she had never really had enough Champagne and now looked forward to enjoying it in vast quantities. Her fiancé promised her that she should certainly have Champagne in abundance – she should even bathe in it.

On their wedding night, in a suite in one of London's luxury hotels, the bride found that the bedroom was literally decorated with Champagne: splits, halves, bottles. They were ranged along the chimney-piece, grouped on the bedside table, pink Champagne in an ice bucket garlanded with roses stood alongside the dressing-table and, when she went into the bathroom, she uttered a cry of delight. There were apparently innumerable bottles ranged all along the side of the marble bath – pints and gallons and quarts of the stuff, waiting to be opened and tipped into the bath in abandon. 'You see,' said the bridegroom, 'I promised – you shall bathe in Champagne!'.

Gaily casting garments aside, the bride hastened to start opening the bottles. (Yes, there were even grippers provided to help her open the bottles.) From the bedroom her husband heard happy laughs as corks popped and popped. After some time she called out 'Come and see me lying in the foam!'

He went into the bathroom, to see her reclining in a mass of golden bubbles, holding one newly-opened bottle high above her head, about to direct its contents onto her beautiful bosom. The bridegroom cried out in delight, exclaimed in love – then, Champagne shipper that he was, he noticed the bottle his lady was holding. He registered the label – the date – he darted forward and seized it with an anguished cry. 'Darling, darling – *not* the vintage!' (And I hope he then reached for the nearest toothmug.)

They did live happily ever after.

The wine game

Ever since people began talking about wine and giving dinner parties, tricks have been played on those who 'drink the label', or, in other words, utter exuberant and often poetic descriptions of wines that they suppose themselves to be drinking or to have drunk. A variation on the tricks attempted on wine snobs is 'the game', played around many hospitable tables, when guests try to work out exactly what wine is being served.

The most famous example of this is certainly Roald Dahl's short story *Taste*, which I shall not spoil by giving here, but only say that the tale turns on a very important prize being the reward of whoever gets the wine right – and proves the point that a glance at the bottle or a good tip to the butler can be most rewarding, if either is possible!

The trial by taste to which each of three possible Lord Peter Wimseys is submitted to determine the genuine article in Dorothy L. Sayers' story, unfortunately falls at the last fence. The Gage d'Or, or supreme test, concerned the real Wimsey's ability to identify 'Napoleon brandy'; this is a very vague reference indeed – unless the intended implication was that Lord Peter identified the Cognac as that of the firm of Courvoisier, whose label bears the motto 'The brandy of Napoleon'.

This is a standard and, therefore, non-vintage Cognac which is widely available. What I think Dorothy Sayers probably meant to indicate was that Lord Peter picked out a vintage Cognac. But it is unlikely that, champion though he was, he would have been able to do so as, even before the French Government forbade the dating of Cognacs, (the market did tend to offer endless supplies of one otherwise excellent firm's '1914') vintage Cognac was rare; certainly I have never known anyone – even the master blenders of the great Cognac establishments – venture to assert that he or she could date the spirit accurately; maybe they'd appraise it 'very old', pick out an establishment's individual house style and, if the spirit were not a blend, the particular region of the defined area from which it came. These features are about as close to absolute identification that anyone, certainly someone outside the wine trade, would be likely to get.

Certainly, if Wimsey were a regular brandy drinker, he should have been able to differentiate between, say, a Courvoisier and a Martell, a Delamain and a Hennessy or an Otard. The slip in the story does tend to make the reader who knows even a little about spirits doubt some of Dorothy Sayers' other statements of fact in certain stories, though usually she seems to have been meticulous in verifying her references. Maybe the drinker whom she consulted for this detail was himself no brandy lover and simply reiterated the old – and still often believed – tale of 'Napoleon brandy'.

It's certainly a fact that, for years after the Battle of Waterloo, odd bottles of wines and, I think, spirits also, would appear in salerooms marked as having been 'brought back from Moscow'; just as old Madeiras used to be labelled 'Rétour des Indes', quite truthfully, when, in cask, they had been used as ballast in the sailing ships travelling to and from the far east, the voyage making a marked improvement on the wine. But 'General Winter' would not have had a benevolent effect on Napoleon's wine commissariat at all, while any spirits would probably have been drunk in desperation, apart from those stashed in Bonaparte's travelling carriage – 'for medicinal purposes' of course.

People who drink labels or go by what the wine card or menu states the wine to be can come seriously unstuck, as I once did when called on to pronounce about a particular claret at a luncheon given by the now defunct Academy of Wine in London. Slightly behind with tasting the wines being served in the course of the meal, I picked up my glass and – in my own defence I must say it – without tasting it, launched into a panegyric on a particular vintage of a particular claret. I was assuming that the vintage was the same as it had been on the previous occasion, a month or so before. But it had been changed – and it was only in the midst of my eulogy of the wine that the secretary, fortunately a friend, broke in to tell me that the vintage was quite different and that I was all wrong!

One should never be too sure of oneself. But one should never give way if convinced that one is right, either. Many years ago I was at a dinner given by the late Allan Sichel in his house in Hampstead, in which there were present a number of wine lovers, also a great wine merchant. As the junior at the table, I was on the host's left and required to speak first on the quality of a Burgundy that, after several preliminary fine wines, was poured from a decanter into our glasses. On such an occasion it was reasonable to assume that the wines would all be exceptional, as those that had gone before this one had been. However, although extremely nervous, I felt I must say that I didn't like the wine and why. My neighbour on the left, the next to speak, raved about this 'marvellous old wine' and so did everybody around the table – except for that great wine merchant, the late Ronald Avery, who, more polite than I, mentioned that he thought there was, 'something not quite right, you know, old boy,' about it. The decanter came back to the host, who smacked his hand down on the table and proclaimed, 'This wine is absolutely undrinkable – and you', pointing to the man on my left who had said how wonderful it was, 'are to finish

the decanter and will not get anything else. You,' to me, 'will go down to the cellar and put your hand along the bin in such-and-such a place, pulling out the first bottle you find. Bring it up.'

What we had been drinking was the 1919 Clos Vougeot, which had definitely 'gone off' with age. What I, obeying instructions, put my hand on in the bin was the 1911 Clos Vougeot, which I brought up (praying that I should not stumble on the steps) and which the host then opened and poured from the bottle. It was one of the wines I shall always remember. That was the reward for speaking the truth.

Two other stories show the advisability of complete honesty. I was a guest at a dinner in the north of England, to which the host also invited an eminent member of the port shippers, Cockburn. At the end of dinner two decanters were circulated, both of them, according to the host, the same vintage of Cockburn port. The other trade guest said no, when the second decanter reached him – this was not a Cockburn port. The host insisted. It had been ordered, it must have been Cockburn, like the other bottle. The guest went on to affirm that this was not and never could have been a Cockburn wine. I was quite lost at this stage, but could tell that each was individual. The wine waiter was summoned. Yes, he admitted, something had seemed amiss with the second bottle of Cockburn when he had decanted the wines – so he had substituted the vintage port of another establishment . . .

CUTTING!

· Host. "WHAT BIN DID YOU PUT THAT MARSALA IN, MUGGLES?"
New Butler. "IN THE—AH—DUST-BIN, SIR!!"

Cartoon indicating the hazards of wine service. Jokes about wine recur in 19th century novels and periodicals.

The classic story about this sort of thing has been told many times, but it's a good one. A character, who sounds as if he might have been rather malicious, invited a man supposed to be experienced in wine to dine and sleep at his country house. The dinner and the wines were on a magnificent scale and when the port, already decanted, was produced, the host asked the guest if he knew what it was. The guest appraised the wine, ventured an opinion as to shipper and vintage. So did the other diners.

The host then said how silly they all were – for this particular port had been bought that morning. He'd sent his chauffeur to the local village grocer and the wine was put into a magnificent decanter to see whether anybody would be beguiled by the ceremony with which it was surrounded. Discomforture of guest? Not quite. He reiterated his opinion and, the following morning, went to the village shop and asked about the supplies of port. Yes, they had some few old bottles, not particularly expensive, which the gentleman was free to inspect. The gentleman did inspect them – and made an offer way above the shop price for the lot. For he'd been right. The port was a magnificent vintage from a great shipper and it had been sold off on the side to the shop by his host's butler. The previous morning the chauffeur had simply gone down to the shop and bought back some of the contents of the port bin!

Of course, it has been rightly remarked, if somebody knows he or she is going to be made to 'play', a decent tip to the butler or maid can be worth more than a look at the wine's label. Seeing the cork, or even just the capsule can be a definite clue, if not an actual giveaway – many fine wines today have branded corks and sometimes designs on the capsules.

Knowing the sort of wines stocked by the merchant from whom your host usually buys can also be a guideline – though of course he may have deliberately shopped elsewhere so as to mislead you. And today, when the continent, rather than just the country of origin, has to be considered in tasting a wine 'blind', the possibilities make the game more complicated. But it can be played successfully. I have been present when people have gone straight through a set of wines served at a dinner and identified each one correctly (I've even managed two or three in a row myself on rare occasions) – and I've also known the same respected authorities be twenty or thirty years astray when trying to divine vintage. Indeed, I remember one grower who, tasting with a blindfold over his eyes, announced that his wine – a particularly fine red Beaujolais – was actually a white wine! So, the ability to 'taste blind' is not just a fiction, but neither is it the be all and end all of tasting; obviously, if you have never tasted a particular wine at all you're unlikely to identify it and if, for some reason, a wine that you do know well has been made somewhat differently, you may be excused for not recognising it.

One of the silliest boasts is that, 'I can tell claret from Burgundy'. Ho hum. In theory, you should not confuse a red Burgundy, made solely from the Pinot Noir grape, with a claret that must be a mixture of several different sorts of grapes, not including the Pinot Noir. But people do mistake Burgundy for claret and claret for Burgundy. Indeed, if somebody sees a red wine being poured out of a square-shouldered bottle of the shape associated with Bordeaux, they may – if they know the pourer is a claret-lover – assume that the wine is claret. If you doubt that anybody can be so easily influenced by appearances, try offering the 'connoisseurs' or 'experts' among your wine-minded friends a red wine poured out of a green Mosel bottle, or a white wine out of a (well-rinsed) bottle that has obviously contained port. You'll be surprised at what some suppose the wines to be!

Another wine game providing much enjoyment is the Australian 'Options'. This is fun because it can be played by both the experienced and absolute beginners. The host or hostess pours the wine, then asks the company to choose from three 'options' about it, one of which must be true. For example, the question might be, 'Is this wine from Australia, California or France?' Round the table, quickly, each diner opts for one of the three. When all have spoken, the host says who is right – and, if people play for money, an agreed stake goes into a jackpot. Then the next question, 'Is it mainly Cabernet Sauvignon, Pinot Noir, Syrah?' Eventually the wine is identified. Of course, people who are shy of venturing can follow the opinion of someone who is supposed to know; others simply speak up. The important thing is that there should be no stopping and thinking because, as has been scientifically established, the perceptions involved with tasting slacken and concentration becomes weak after a matter of seconds, so speed is wise anyway when tasting seriously. The first impression is so often the right one!

Of course, there are the people who deliberately try to mislead others. I've been informed that I was going to be given a red Burgundy – and only after I'd expressed considerable doubt, did the host triumphantly tell me it was a claret. (There's nothing profitable in this – unless you want to make an enemy, because nobody likes being made to seem foolish.) And there are the people who, also deliberately, spoil wines that are to be presented for serious appraisal. This is knife work of the most cunning kind. The wrong apéritif can make the first course wine taste less good than it should, the inappropriate food can dowse the delicacy of a 'fine and rare' bottle, the courses preceding what should be 'the' wine of the meal may have excoriated the palate . . .

Some years ago a group of very important business magnates were invited to visit Bordeaux – private jet, hospitality at its most discreetly lavish in several great châteaux, foods of a sort to make even the most pampered tastebuds perk up, cooked by chefs of international repute. And wines which were the treasures of the *bibliothèques* or 'libraries' (where the old fine wines are stored) of the estates. Each meal was programmed as a symphony of gastronomy.

One grand estate had not been able to entertain the visitors to luncheon or dinner for some reason. But, once the tour had been worked out – the organisers throughout the Gironde sweated as they timed the journeys in

above right *Where the most important work in wine begins – the samples are ranged in the tasting rooms and the buyers appraise each one in quiet, clean, wholly 'unpicturesque' lab-like conditions.*

below right *In the cellars of the Hospices de Beaune, buyers attending the sale have a prior tasting, offering their tastevins to receive the samples. It can be cold in November, which is why they are well wrapped up.*

left *Examining samples in Portugal – those working in the tasting room often wear white coats, both as a protection from splashes and so that no colouring from their clothes is reflected on the wine.*

below A barco rabelo, *the shallow vessel formerly in use for bringing the casks of wine down from the upper reaches of the Douro to Vila Nova de Gaia and the shippers' lodges. Great adroitness was necessary for the boatmen to manoeuvre the vessel through the rapidly-running narrows with the single oar. Today, several firms maintain boats moored off Gaia for publicity purposes but it has not been possible to use them up river since the various dams were built.*

limousines between château and château, luxury hotel and triple-Michelin-starred restaurant – the owner of this great property expressed the wish to offer at least a *vin d'honneur* of his own personal Champagne to the visitors for a quarter of an hour on the château terrace. The owner of the estate where the subsequent and final luncheon was to be taken objected that the alteration in the schedule was impossible: there would be no time, the delay would ruin the menu, the provision of the apéritif – by someone to whom he was always sleekly polite in public but whom he really didn't consider a friend – dittoed what he would have offered. The organisers, wishing to please both great men, swore that not one second over the time would be taken – they would get the party to luncheon on the dot. So it was agreed.

On the morning of the luncheon, the owner of the estate where the final meal was to be served went down to the kitchen to study the pre-arranged menu. It should be noted that, as is often usual on such occasions, the host's wine was to be served before the wine of the neighbouring property; the latter wine had been planned to be the star and climax of the meal, all the more so as its proprietor had been unable to entertain the party, except briefly. Knowing the wine, I can say it certainly would have been unforgettable. The luncheon host hadn't objected – he had, after all, succeeded in getting the entire party to *his* house for the meal; his wines and *his* preprandial Champagne (each of them had his own) would, he had thought, make more of an impression than any others anyway. This was before the arrangement about the vin d'honneur elsewhere.

The menu was originally one of those simple but superb compositions, the several great clarets being programmed up to a magnificent dish of lamb for which the Pauillac region is famous. The wine of the neighbouring estate would accompany the lamb, being the third red wine and the last one before any cheese.

'I think I'll change the menu,' announced the host, looking his cook straight in the eyes. 'We'll have curried chicken with the Château . . .'

So they did. And if anyone managed to taste the exquisite, subtle, gently lingering claret that would have made such an impression accompanying the *agneau de Pauillac*, I should be very surprised.

It's seldom, however, that wine actually provokes maliciousness and – although I've certainly heard furious arguments about various wines in all parts of the world – I've never known anybody arise and brain someone with a bottle, so it may be counted as a civilising commodity. Indeed, the conversation around a table of wine lovers can be as enjoyable as the beverage. One took place years before I was born, when some very senior members of the wine trade and my own beloved teacher, Allan Sichel, then a very young man, were trying to work out what the two wines were in the decanters circulating before them. A variety of opinions was put forward. Eventually the host announced, 'Gentlemen, you have been discussing two halves of the same magnum.' 'Then,' said Allan Sichel 'mine, sir, was the half nearest the cork.'

Drink and diplomacy

'If you're given Champagne at lunch, there's a catch somewhere,' said Lord Lyons, who was British Ambassador in Paris from 1867–1887.

He does not, indeed, sound gastronomically inclined or very wine minded; Lady Gladwyn, the Ambassadress from 1954–1960, comments in *The Paris Embassy*, (Collins 1976), 'his hard-driven staff, who often went without lunch, staggered exhausted, at seven in the evening to revive themselves with the new habit of cocktails, and frequently had to return to the Chancery till past midnight'. I cannot trace the source of this most interesting early reference to cocktails, but perhaps it is a covering phrase for brandy and soda, gin and bitters (somewhat down the social scale) or, even, Champagne.

However, many ententes have been made more cordial over the dining tables of the past, and many constructive policies have been planned, for surroundings that are elegant and spacious are conducive to clear thinking and a civilised approach to life. Anyone who has seen the beautiful, lofty dining-room of Sir Robert Walpole's town house, in which the first Cabinet meeting was held in the early 18th century, will appreciate that those meeting there, whether or not they had a glass before them, would approach the problems of government in a calm, benign manner. By comparison, the Cabinet Room of Number 10 Downing Street is crowded and cluttered, with scant space behind the chairs and the chairs themselves so close together that the boarding school objuration to, 'Keep your elbows to yourself!' may be muttered. Very often the feelings of those shut up there must veer from an aggressive and oppressed wish to get out and doubt as to whether it will ever be possible to do so.

Until Napoleon I broke up the 1815 Congress of Vienna by escaping from Elba, the Congress, which, according to the Prince de Ligne (1735–1814), gave parties rather than getting on with settling the peace ('Le congrès ne marche pas, il danse') enjoyed refreshments from some of the most distinguished chefs of the time, each delegate vying to excel in the provision of food and wines. Talleyrand, somewhat at a disadvantage at the outset, had an invaluable ally in the great Antonin Carême (1784–1833) who directed his kitchens. The compliments exchanged between heads of state on this occasion are often quoted in connection with the wines of the different countries represented, but in the context they're not, perhaps, to be taken as serious and critical expressions of appreciation. Metternich, for example, crafty diplomat that he was, had once tried to ingratiate himself with Napoleon who, totally ungastronomic, and hardly a connoisseur of wine either, had remarked politely on Metternich's estate, Schloss Johannisberg. At this Metternich replied that Napoleon had an even finer wine in France – the Château Chalon of the Jura. (Although it is quite impossible to compare the two wines.) It is not easy to imagine Talleyrand and the French contingent truly preferring a non-French wine on any occasion. But diplomacy spoke.

In the 18th century, Madeira had become of particular interest to those living in what were then the North American Colonies of Great Britain; the British insisted that all goods imported by North America should be transported by 'British Bottoms', (British ships) to the advantage of the British merchants. But the island of Madeira, way out in the Atlantic, could supply wine to ships of other nations, which would then take it on to the colonies. It proved a popular and comparatively inexpensive drink.

Up until the middle of the 18th century, it had been an accepted practice for customs officers throughout North America to allow merchants bringing in goods to enter only part of their cargo in the customs' books, the remainder being landed without paying duty. In 1765, however, the Stamp Act, putting further pressure on the inhabitants, began to incense those 'Colonials' still of British nationality.

When, in 1768, the appropriately named sloop 'Liberty' arrived in Boston with a cargo of Madeira, the trade commissioners refused to allow the captain to land half the cargo free of duty, as had been customary. The 'Tide-Waiter', or official who went on board, argued violently with the captain, who then locked him up and proceeded to unload the entire cargo. He was not going to break with what had been established practice! The trade commissioners then sent customs officers down to the harbour to arrest the ship, but this infuriated the large crowd of people there assembled; they saw themselves being balked of any chance of having their cheap wine. They set about the customs officers and burnt the inspector general's boat; both commissioners and customs officials had to take refuge in Castle William, while the people got – and presumably drank – their Madeira. This event preceded the more famous Boston Tea Party and was certainly not as wasteful.

From then on, Madeira was the patriotic drink for North American gentlemen. Noël Cossart, doyen of the

A

CATALOGUE

OF

A VALUABLE AND GENUINE SELECTION OF FINE

MADEIRA, SERCIAL, TENERIFFE,

AND

Malmsey Wines,

IN THE WOOD,

WHICH ARE THE GENUINE PROPERTY OF

A CAPTAIN IN THE BRITISH NAVY,

AND

HAVE HAD THE BENEFIT OF BEING RIPENED AND IMPROVED IN THE WARM CLIMATE OF SOUTH AMERICA, DURING THE PROPRIETOR'S COMMAND ON THAT STATION;

WHICH

Will be Sold by Auction,

By Mr. CHRISTIE,

AT HIS

GREAT ROOM, KING STREET, ST. JAMES'S SQUARE,

On THURSDAY, 10th of JULY, 1828,

AT ONE O'CLOCK, PRECISELY.

SAMPLES OF THE WINES WILL BE PRODUCED AT THE TIME OF SALE.

A sale including the then popular beverage, Madeira, at the auction room that became the world-famous firm of Christie, Manson & Woods.

An 18th century loyalist glass, inscribed 'The King and Friends of His Majesty's American Loyalists'.

Madeira wine trade today, notes that Francis Scott Key (1779–1843), the composer of the *Star Spangled Banner* and Betsy Ross, the lady who sewed the first American Flag, both drank Madeira; so did Benjamin Franklin, Thomas Jefferson, Chief Justice Marshall and Daniel Webster. George Washington is said to have drunk a pint of Madeira wine every day at dinner; it was the wine for the toast at his inauguration when, in 1792, Jefferson decided to make Washington D.C. the capital of the United States. To this day, Madeira is very much a wine for discerning wine lovers in the United States.

But Madeira maintained its popularity in the India of the British Raj. Here it was often referred to as 'S.S.S.', the letters standing for 'Subalterns' Soothing Syrup'. This was a result of the belief that the port traditional in regimental messes was too taxing a drink for the newly-arrived young officer, not yet acclimatised to the country.

Drink and politics became closely associated in the 17th century. In 1688 King James II escaped from London to France in what has since been known as the 'Glorious Revolution'; William of Orange, who had a twofold claim to the English Crown through his Stuart mother, sister of Charles II, and through his wife, Mary, daughter of James II, then arrived in England to replace James. Holland had long been famous for gin – the expression 'Dutch courage' comes from the 16th century when English soldiers drank it to warm them in the wars against Spain in the Netherlands. Although gin became popular because of the advent of 'Dutch

Billy', it was hardly a drink to swig regardless, especially for hours at the end of dinner. The full red wines of the Douro were becoming popular anyway; in 1703 the Methuen Treaty gave preferential treatment to Portuguese wines. So the adherents to the reigning monarch began to consume quantities of port – which is why the Loyal Toast is traditionally drunk in port to this day.

This 18th century glass, showing King William, would have been used to toast success to the Hanoverian cause, in opposition to the Jacobites.

The Jacobites, adherents to the Stuart cause, drank claret, especially in Scotland, where the 'Auld Alliance' Between Scotland and France had established Bordeaux wine for centuries. So that the Jacobites should not reveal themselves as being against the joint sovereigns William and Mary, they would raise their glasses at the time of the Loyal Toast, but unobtrusively pass their hands over any carafe, bowl of water, jug, or section of the wine cooler that often stood on the table. Thus they drank 'To the King' but 'over the water', in other words, to whom they considered the true monarch on the other side of the English Channel, thereby expressing hopes for his restoration. I believe that Jacobite societies follow the custom to this day, just as they put white roses at the foot of the beheaded King Charles I's statue at the top of Whitehall, every January 29th, the anniversary of his execution.

In the reign of Queen Anne and in the subsequent reigns of the Hanoverian monarchs, the Jacobite toast became more sinister: 'To the little gentleman in the velvet coat – coupled with the name of Sorrel.' This phrase would often be muttered after the 'over the water' gesture; it refers to King William's horse, Sorrel, putting his foot in a mole hole and throwing the King – who later died from his injuries – against the pommel. The 'little gentleman in velvet' is the mole, because a mole's coat has no nap.

Victoria and, later, Albert, put an end to the heavy drinking bouts of earlier reigns, including the lengthy postprandial sessions, when various wines circulated on the table and, as Lord Melbourne said with anticipatory enjoyment, the gentlemen could 'talk broad' after the ladies had left the dining-room. One wonders when chamber pots ceased to be kept in sideboards (or even parked in the corner of the dining-room) and who was the last host to keep servants ready to loosen the neckcloths of gentlemen who collapsed under the table and might risk apoplexy.

In many of the great houses of the day and, of course, in the gentlemens' clubs throughout Great Britain, affairs of state and business were still frequently settled over a glass of wine. The 'combination room' or 'common rooms' of some of the colleges of the older universities continue the tradition of drinking after dinner, as will be known to those who have read the C.P. Snow novels (or watched the television adaptation) concerned with semi-political and university machinations for influence and, presumably, affluence. I admit that, in the few episodes I saw on television, the glasses were too small, too cut and seldom of the right shape for the true lovers of wine supposed to be shown. There was even an occasion when a don proposing, 'a Mosel I think might amuse you,' to

A men's dinner in 1830. Note the man-servant loosening the neckcloth of the gentleman under the table.

right George Cruikshank's illustration to a Harrison Ainsworth novel, 'The Miser's Daughter' in which, in about 1744, someone refuses to drink the health of the King – 'over the water', creating reactions anticipating the famous H.M. Bateman cartoons of 'The man who . . .' perpetuated some social gaffe.

somebody whom he hoped to induce to vote for a particular candidate, indicated a pale, square-shouldered bottle that had a look of one from which a dry white Bordeaux would be poured, instead of the elongated green bottle from which a Mosel would emanate.

Certainly, drinkers of today, in this sort of setting, follow their own preferences, in no way defining their politics or asserting their allegiance by the wine they drink. The choice, however, would have been much more significant and serious in the past.

The honouring of a health was important, indicating who owed allegiance to whom. In medieval times violence was easily aroused between the partisans of different religions, of one baron or overlord and another, or between the inhabitants of one town and another. (Maybe the violence associated with some so-called 'sporting' events is similar to that which caused an early ban on wearing swords in the dining-hall.)

Today the 'Loyal Toast' means the toast to the sovereign, but the very word 'loyal' is important historically. Traditionally, this is the first toast or health drunk by the company assembled, who rise to 'honour' it, as they do when toasting the health of a head of state on official occasions. It is the office, rather than the individual, whose health is drunk in this context.

I shall never forget the expression on the faces of a group of aggressively anti-Gaullist wine growers when, at a luncheon in the Graves district of Bordeaux at which our host had pro-

posed the health of Her Majesty the Queen, the leader of the British party enthusiastically leaped to his feet and asked us to drink the health of 'The Général de Gaulle!', instead of the 'President of the Republic'. (But the company courteously rose and drank.)

Apart from anything else, usually it is simpler to get one's tongue around the title – President, or whatever – than the sort of name that can, on a British tongue, cause a tactless mispronunciation. So, if in doubt, use the name of the office rather than the person, should you be faced with this situation.

There are two exceptions to the custom of the company rising for the Loyal Toast to the sovereign. Once, a monarch who was dining aboard ship, rose with the company to honour the toast and bumped his head on a beam. Since that time the Royal Navy remains seated for the ceremony. Opinions differ as to which king it was that started this tradition, but William IV, the 'Sailor King', would probably have been aware of the hazards of low ceilings. Some people suggest George III, but others, and I tend to agree with them, opt for 'Prinny', the Regent, later George IV, whose alcoholic intake was usually considerable, and who might very well have forgotten that he was neither in Carlton House Terrace nor the Brighton Pavilion when rising to his feet after a lavish repast aboard ship.

Many will know of the Royal Navy tradition, but there's an even older one.

The benchers of Lincoln's Inn, one of the Inns of Court, have been famous for centuries both for their hospitality and their entertainments. One of them informed me that when his predecessors invited King Charles II and his court to dine with them in the 17th century, the Merry Monarch and the rest of the company were literally incapable of getting to their feet to drink the Loyal Toast – so Lincoln's Inn honours the Loyal Toast seated to this day. Mention has been made (page 16) of the special toasting glasses, with stems so slim that they could be snapped easily between the fingers to prevent any less worthy toast ever being drunk from the same vessels. Exuberant diners would also sometimes hurl their glasses to the floor or into the fire.

In recent times, at any rate in the UK, it has become customary after the Loyal Toast, and any toast to a head of state that may also be drunk on formal occasions, for the toast master to announce that the company may smoke. Here I admit that, although I used to smoke after dinner myself and have been surrounded by smokers all my life, including those who have taught me about wine, I cannot approve of the Loyal Toast always being drunk early in the meal, with permission to smoke being assumed from that time on.

The present Prime Minister, the Right Honourable Mrs Margaret Thatcher, MP, recently made an important speech before the beginning of a dinner, as she had then to leave to attend the House of Commons. A friend who was present told me that clouds of cigarette smoke almost concealed the smoked salmon at the opening of the meal. I should have liked to cancel any wine if I'd been there!

There are, however, special circumstances that may require a modification of the tradition. In his life of Earl Mountbatten, (Collins, 1985), Philip Ziegler relates that General Eisenhower, on being posted to Britain during World War II, explained that, being a chainsmoker, he would not be able to endure any of the formal dinners and luncheons that he might be required to attend as Commander in Chief. Mountbatten, with complete practicality, said this could be dealt with – and, at the first occasion when the Loyal Toast was to have been drunk, Mountbatten himself rose to propose this and other formal toasts immediately after the soup. So all went well.

It might perhaps seem more sensible to drink the Loyal Toast during the apéritif before the meal begins, if people care so little about what they eat and drink that they wish to blow smoke over it regardless. In case people suppose me to be too severe, I can only ask – would they enjoy a meal at which I, seated at their table, used a deodorant, a hairspray or, in accordance with the conventions of other civilisations' manners, expressed my enjoyment by belching and farting? Besides, if a meal is intended for the enjoyment of a gathering in which many people may not smoke at all, then why should their enjoyment have to be clouded?

It may be a surprise to know that there are some people who consider it discourteous to drink the Loyal Toast in anything except an alcoholic beverage, very much as their ancestors might have resented a Jacobite guest surreptitiously passing a glass over the water jug.

The important thing is that the toast *is* 'honoured' and that the company actually drinks – touching one's lips to the glass without consuming anything might, certainly at one time, have been considered disloyal. I think the most charming example of diplomacy in relation to drink that I know occurred when the head of a much respected world organisation, whose members are total abstainers, was invited to be the guest of honour at the annual banquet of another world organisation, whose members are certainly not averse to enjoying all the good things of life, including wine. The guest of honour asked advice in advance; of course, the hosts were only too willing to provide him with a non-alcoholic drink, but he explained that he did not wish to honour the toast to the Queen in orange juice, as this, he thought, might parade his principles in a pharisaical manner. The wine merchant supplying the banquet therefore arranged for a carafe of black grape juice to be set in front of the guest's place; all concerned apparently had great fun ensuring that the colour of the grape juice should exactly match the tone of the Burgundy and port that everyone else was drinking.

This displays a far more civilised and courteous attitude than that of the wife of one of the British Ambassadors in Paris. The then Comptroller of the household, the late dear Colonel Andrew Graham, told me how, in the superb setting of the house of Pauline Borghese, Napoleon's sister, in a dining-room displaying the finest silver, glass and china, a rare Champagne was poured into the crystal glass set before each place at the end of one particular meal. The Ambassadress didn't even taste the wine, but, collecting the ladies as she rose from her place, swept them all from the room. My informant admitted that he then enjoyed the untouched wine from the glasses of the ladies on either side of him.

W.....and omen

'Women and wine should life employ,' sings Macheath, the highwayman in John Gay's Beggar's Opera (1728), and later insists, 'I must have women. There is nothing unbends the mind like them.' Whether this is so or not, the association of women with wine seems always to have existed, sometimes in practical as well as social ways.

In ancient Babylonia only women were allowed to keep the taverns; some commentators suppose that the type of establishment referred to was a brothel and therefore the woman tavern keeper was the madam in charge. But this seems to be an opinion, rather than anything supported by facts and I do not see why the women who ran the taverns should not have been perfectly efficient in their work, coping with the various laws then in force controlling the sale of liquor, which included the taverner being thrown into pond, lake or sea if she gave short measure. Anyone who has seen a woman controlling a bar, a restaurant, a club, even those frequented by a fairly tough, predominantly masculine clientèle, can easily imagine that these Babylonian ladies would have been up to their work.

The extraordinary ceremonies in ancient Greece involving women of all classes, from the highest to the lowest, rushing off to the woods to celebrate Bacchic rites in honour of the God of Wine, are apparently true events – not mere legends. Euripides relates in *The Bacchae* how, in the course of these excitements, the women tear to pieces the unfortunate Pentheus, who, impelled by a natural curiosity, has followed them. If the women really did kill those who spied on them, the concept is very difficult to understand. Edward Hyams, in his wonderful book *Dionysus, A Social History of the Wine Vine* (Thames & Hudson 1965), explains this Bacchic raging, when the people are possessed by the god, as a feeling that 'is not merriness; it is not human at all; it is the joy one observes in a cat or a fox or the kind of wild play which ends not in an embrace but in a killing'.

It seems a convoluted theory and, although I am normally the last person to bring into any discussion the argument that the masculine point of view is imposed on women, it is perhaps pertinent to remark that Euripides was a man and so was Mr Hyams. Although *The Bacchae* is supposed to contain some beautiful poetry and although women are certainly capable of violence and extreme cruelty, the subject is one that I have never begun to understand; could it even be a masculine argument against allowing women to drink? An Awful Warning – 'If you drink wine, my dear Penelope, you simply don't know what you're letting yourself in for!' 'Darling Odysseus, I just got into the habit while you were away all those years.'

Even today, some find a drunken woman far more distasteful than a drunk man, yet certainly women must have been involved with wine in early times, even if they were only employed, like the children were, to go out and scare the birds off the vines. As for those women who, however subordinate their role might be in law, had to oversee the running of their husbands' property, vineyards included, while the men were jollying away at the wars, they would not have been wholly ignorant of making wine, if only to ensure that any steward or agent who remained behind was not cheating his master. Nor does there seem to have been any shocked reaction to Book IV of Homer's *Odyssey*, in which Helen adds to the bowl in which the wine was mixed (as it always was at that time) 'a drug that had the power of robbing grief and anger of their sting and banishing all painful memories . . . this powerful anodyne . . . had been given by an Egyptian lady'.

True, in ancient Rome, Romulus, one of the two (legendary) founders of the City, approved the law that prohibited women and even men under thirty to drink wine; a Roman obviously of the most austere traditions, Egnatius Mecenius, sent his wife to draw wine for him and, when he saw that she had drunk some – one longs to know whether he had somehow marked the previous level on the relevant amphora like those people who used to mark the levels on decanters, or whether she, trying to please, drank to his health in front of him – knocked her down and killed her. Mecenius was said to have been highly commended by Romulus for this action. But one cannot take such stories wholly seriously. They may have been invented to awe recalcitrant wives, just as so many fairy tales have been made up to frighten children into good behaviour.

Marcus Terentius Varro (116–27 BC) first librarian of Rome's great library, author of more than six hundred books, was eighty years old when he wrote one of the few works that survive him – *De Re Rustica* – so as to provide a manual of guidance to his wife, in running the farm that she had just bought. I do not believe Signora Varro didn't sample her own wine.

Mark Anthony gave Cleopatra the island of Cyprus, because of its wine, though I cannot find any reference to that Egyptian lady being particularly wine-minded – one does not associate connoisseurship with the habit of throwing pearls into a cup of wine and then drinking the liquid when the pearl has dissolved, albeit to prolong youth. The semi-magical, life-prolonging properties of certain precious metals, notably gold, were a very early tradition; flecks of gold leaf still glitter in at least one liqueur and the sweetmeats prepared for renowned guests in many eastern countries may be powdered or even coated with gold. The person who buys an expensive box of chocolates with the odd touch of gold on the *couverture* (chocolate covering) of some of the contents is, without realising it, doing the same thing as the quaffers of pearlised potions. But there are no elixirs of life.

In the dark ages and the early medieval period, it is reasonable to suppose that the ladies who ran the great houses and estates, or who were in charge of large communities of religious, would have at least supervised the making of wine, even if they did not make it themselves. Certainly, everything within doors, including the brewhouse, wine and cider presses, the still room and pharmacy would have been part of the domain of the lady of the house, or, in a convent, of the abbess or her cellarer. Men might possibly have been employed in female religious establishments for some of the rougher tasks, although I do not suppose that the work would have been beyond a sturdy young country woman; some of the girls I have seen working in wineries in the southern hemisphere, especially Australia, have done so with complete competence and expertise. And I've seen a young woman in an English vineyard pick up and carry three cases of wine with ease.

I should give much to know of any involvement in wine by the beautiful and fascinating heiress of Aquitaine, Duchess Aliénor or Eleanor, who, after divorcing the King of France, married the Count of Anjou, Henry Plantagenet, in 1152, and became Queen of England in 1154. Her duchy, extending from the Loire to the Pyrenees and reaching over into Burgundy, where the great Abbey of Cluny was founded by her grandfather, included some of what are the finest vineyards in France today, and the English court's enjoyment of claret established a liking for the red wines of Bordeaux that has persisted ever since. Eleanor's beauty and charm inspired extravagant verses from the troubadours; these qualities were reinforced by her wit, ability in administration and remarkable stamina, which enabled her to resist the rigours of imprisonment, to travel at great speed and escape many dangers by her courage and toughness. Even as quite an old woman she escaped from one of her husband's castles by sliding down a rope into a snowy night and, when a dowager, she brought Princess Berengaria of Navarre out to Cyprus to marry Richard, her favourite. Unfortunately the 'Lion Heart' didn't inherit his mama's healthy sensuality and seems to have preferred the company of men – all those tournaments and crusades were no doubt responsible.

A professional woman who certainly understood the medicinal value of wine was Trotula, sometimes known as Madam Trot. She was a Doctor of the medieval School of Salerno, which was open to women students, and she wrote a number of books, including some on obstetrics and cosmetic hygiene, her remedies in many instances involving wine. Salvatore P. Lucia, of the University of California School of Medicine, in *A History of Wine as Therapy* (Lippincott 1963) quotes Trotula's prescriptions for infant coughs, burns and chaps, foul breath during pregnancy and prolapsed uterus after childbirth, all of them including wine.

In *Le Menagier de Paris*, written around 1393 by a Parisian for the guidance of his wife, there are many references to the care and preservation of wine, suggesting that the young housewife, although she might have several servants, had to take a personal interest in, and exercise supervision over, the wine used for various household occasions. It should not be forgotten that those households able to eat reasonably well on most days also opened the doors of their kitchens to those less fortunate on festivals; provision had to be made for such 'extras' and of course people delivering goods probably got some snack, very much as they might be given a cup of tea today.

In vintage scenes or representations of vineyards, both in illuminated manuscripts and tapestries of these times, women are seen working alongside men in the vineyards and helping to make the wine indoors. To

above right *Age is no deterrent to grape picking at Fleurie in the Beaujolais.*

below right *The vintage in the Barossa Valley, South Australia.*

this day, in vineyard regions, this shared task of cultivation may be seen, not merely at vintage time, but throughout the year. In Alsace, for example, and in many other vineyards, it's a mainly female workforce that, in spring, ties the vines to the wires that support them – 36 kilometres of wire being used for every hectare of vines; imagine this task having to be peformed with twine or twists of straw! And in World War I it was the women, with children and old men, who had to cultivate the vineyards; in Champagne many were actually killed under fire while picking the 1914 vintage; in the cellars of Reims, where the entire population lived during the 1,051 days of the bombardment, the women coped with the wine making as well.

It would be pleasant to associate Queen Elizabeth I with wine in some way, but, as far as I can discover, she ate and drank very moderately indeed, sometimes drinking metheglin, a type of mead flavoured with herbs or spices, maybe as a tactful gesture to her metheglin-drinking Welsh forbears, the Tudors. She seldom actually dined in public, although she did preside at official dinners and banquets. Her terrible childhood and

above left *Madame Clicquot-Ponsardin, the original 'Champagne widow' in her impressive prime.*

below left *Dona Antonia de Ferreira (1810–1886), head of the great port house, elegant even in old age.*

appalling adolescence would certainly not have laid the foundations for a good digestion; the headaches, sickness, diarrhoea and sudden collapses to which she was prone all her life, in spite of her astonishing nervous energy – which always takes its toll in the end – may all be noticed today in people of a certain temperament and creativity. I myself think that Elizabeth Tudor possibly suffered from some form of migraine.

Mary Queen of Scots certainly did drink wine. One of the most charming compliments was paid to her seemingly transparent complexion, when it was said that, as she drank red wine, the rosy tone could be seen as it passed down her throat. Certainly preferable to experiencing a sudden unbecoming flush as the result of an unexpectedly strong drink!

People who are obliged to eat in public a great deal are not usually able to develop much interest in food or drink, simply because so much of what they are obliged to consume is of such insipidity and indifferent quality. Catering on a large scale is, at best, likely to result in food that may be eaten or toyed with rather than savoured. Although these days the wines listed as having been served to royalty and important personages are usually fine, a detailed appreciation of wine is hardly possible when one is surrounded by a large crowd, with demands constantly made on the attention, as well as the hazard of evil tongues, only too ready to publicise any indication of amounts consumed.

In Pommery's establishment in Reims in the 19th century, teams of women would label and pack the bottles. This was common in many installations and to this day it is often women who work on the labelling and packing lines, even though many of the processes are now done by machine.

right Snipping off any rotten or unripe grapes in Alsace, protected by the sun bonnet traditional in many wine regions in former times.

We are occasionally told that the ladies of our own royal family drink a light German wine – sometimes hock is specified – which, like Queen Victoria, they enjoy. But what sort of preference could they form in conjunction with those innumerable public meals in which, I fear, the plasticised chicken, the overcooked cutlet, the soggy salmon, feature far too frequently? The various clerks to the Royal Cellars whom I have known have, of course, been silent as to what 'They' eat on private occasions, when we ordinary people can choose from all kinds of dishes, varying from 'cuisine' to bangers and mash, but I do hope that the royal ladies, whose country estates yield prime produce of every sort, sometimes crack a bottle of something truly 'fine and rare', as the wine auction catalogues say, and that they enjoy this as well.

In the reign of James I (of England and Scotland) his Queen, Anne of Denmark – a country already famous for its consumption of liquor – is on several occasions reported to have been definitely tipsy at various parties at Court. After the Restoration of Charles II in 1660, however, the 'Merry Monarch' and his Court were introduced to the delights of Champagne. This was the result of the Marquis de St-Evremond's arrival in England after his exile by Louis XIV. St-Evremond was one of the founders of the Ordre des Coteaux, a group of influential young nobles, most of them with estates in Champagne. So the Marquis arranged for his favourite drink, mainly the wine of his friend the Marquis de Sillery, to be sent over to London, and bottled here. This was when the British began their long love affair with the lively wine and it's a pleasant thought that 'sweet Nell of Old Drury', Nell Gwynn, who began her career by selling oranges, may actually have made the first version of what was later to become Bucks Fizz: Champagne and orange juice, before it was officially made at Buck's Club in London in 1921.

Lady Mary Wortley Montagu (1689–1762) a beautiful, witty woman, of considerable intelligence, as is shown by her advocacy of inoculation against smallpox, which she had learned about while in

Turkey, refers to 'Champagne and a chicken' as forming part of a supper of reconciliation between lovers who have quarrelled during a party. She certainly could have anticipated Madame de Pompadour's comment that Champagne is the only wine that leaves a woman as beautiful after drinking it as before. But the Marquise, charming though she sounds, as exquisite as was her taste in decor, theatricals, all sorts of 'menus plaisirs' – the 'little delights' that held the attention of Louis XV even when his Bourbon sexuality required frequent satisfaction elsewhere – the 'sincère et tendre Pompadour', as Voltaire called her, was not wine-minded. She ate truffles and celery so as to pep herself up to satisfy Louis XV, and, for all I know, far more unpleasant concoctions. She inspired great works of art in porcelain – yet where are the masterpieces of glass (for wine) that could have been in constant use at her supper tables? She might well have solved many of her problems had the French Court drunk more wine – especially Champagne – and bothered less about the idiotic details of protocol, that permitted nobles to urinate on the staircases of Versailles, or princesses to have enemas administered in public, but not to 'powder their noses' if out picnicking with the monarch.

Queen Henrietta Maria seems to have been uninterested in food and drink, rather oddly for the daughter of Marie de Medici (who is said to have had a sweet tooth) and Henry of Navarre, (who is said to have had his baby lips rubbed with garlic and moistened with Jurançon wine and who announced his wish that every Frenchman might enjoy a chicken in the pot regularly). Perhaps his daughter felt above such mundane matters or, maybe, she didn't care for wine when pregnant, which she frequently was. In her early exile to France the poor woman might not have been able to afford wine. Her sister-in-law, the gorgeous 'Queen of Hearts', Elizabeth, certainly appreciated it when she could afford it, or was given it by any of her numerous admirers.

It was during the 18th century that the white wines of Château Carbonnieux in the Graves, then in the ownership of the Benedictines of Sainte-Croix in Bordeaux, where previously only red wines appear to have been made, came into prominence. An export market was unexpectedly developed for this wine in Constantinople, because a beautiful Bordeaux maiden, captured by pirates, was delivered to the Sultan's seraglio, where she became first favourite. The indulgent Sultan, asking her if there was anything she lacked, was delighted to procure what she said was the basis of her loveliness, her favourite 'mineral water' – white Carbonnieux. Apparently the monks of Sainte-Croix shipped quantities of the wine, referring to it always as 'mineral water of Carbonnieux'. The Sultan expressed astonishment that anyone could want to drink wine (prohibited by the Koran), when they could have such delicious mineral water!

Now begins the great era of the ladies of Champagne, often referred to as 'Champagne widows', because most of their achievements took place after the

deaths of their husbands. First and foremost in the early history of the supreme sparkling wine, is Madame Clicquot.

One of the 'little suppers' given during the Regency period in 18th century France. The company is using elongated flûte glasses to drink Champagne. At these occasions, servants disappeared early in the meal, courses sometimes being served by tables rising through the floor.

Nicole-Barbe Ponsardin married François Clicquot in 1798. They were actually married in a cellar, as the churches in Reims had been deconsecrated during the French Revolution. Widowed in 1806, when she was only twenty-seven, Nicole-Barbe took over the company and although she was certainly fortunate in her associates, especially the colleague who established

Clicquot in Imperial Russia, it was to her conscientiousness and dynamism that the prosperity of the house was due. She worked unremittingly, wandering through the cellars at night, planning how to improve the quality of her wine. And it is said that the first *pupitres* (the wooden frames in which the bottles are turned and shaken so that the deposit descends onto the first cork), were evolved by her from the cut up trestle tables from her own kitchen. Her business activities were not confined to wine; she was respected in many fields and her charitable works were considerable. When she died at the age of eighty-nine, in 1866, she was a revered and loved European personality. And there was very little about making Champagne with which she was not thoroughly familiar.

Madame Pommery, widowed at the age of thirty nine in 1858, had not, as far as is known, previously been actively concerned with her husband's business, but, like Madame Clicquot, she enjoyed the help of an ideal and adept colleague, Monsieur Greno. It was he who persuaded Louise Pommery to concentrate on making sparkling Champagne instead of the red still wine of Champagne, which had previously been the firm's speciality. Madame Pommery evolved a motto in her early days in business which governed all her business life – 'Qualité d' abord'. Madame Pommery's attractive portrait certainly makes her an advertisement for the qualities of champagne. Her courage when her own house was occupied by the Prussians during the war of 1870 is astonishing. She built impressive premises for the firm and a superb park in Reims. Pommery's success in the British market was enormous, but I can find no foundation for the tradition – although folk memory is sometimes more accurate than is supposed – that during the late Victorian and Edwardian shooting parties cries of 'Boy!' would sound from the butts, to attract bottle baskets holding the Prince of Wales' favourite Champagne, Pommery. Yet I've always known Pommery to be 'The Boy', whereas Clicquot has always and rather obviously been 'The Widow'.

Nearer our own time, the late Madame Olry Roederer took over her husband's business in Reims when he died. This she was in some ways equipped to do, by previously having worked as his assistant in the firm. One of her enthusiasms was for breeding champion trotting horses. When she attended any of the events in which her horses took part, dressed with the elegance that is unique to France and adorned with impressive jewels, she too was a magnificent advertisement for Champagne.

Madame Odette Pol Roger, one of the beautiful sisters who, descendants of Sir Richard Wallace, were nicknamed the 'Wallace Collection', has been one of the most successful ambassadors for Champagne that the world has ever known; Sir Winston Churchill, whose favourite wine this was, once remarked 'My dear, I can see the bubbles in your hair!' When he died, Madame Pol Roger put a black band on the label of the Champagne, which it bears to this day.

As famous, but in a different way, is the late Madame Lily Bollinger – 'Tante Lily' both to members of her family and affectionately among many Champenois. She took over the firm on the death of her husband in 1941, a period of appalling difficulties, which she surmounted by a genius for hard work and immense personal charm and dignity. Not merely did she supervise every detail of the business, but, on her bicycle, constantly inspected the vineyards for several hours before getting to her desk at nine in the morning.

In 1968 she was the first lady to be a guest of the Wine & Spirit Association of Great Britain's annual Benevolent Association banquet, to which, until quite recently, women were not invited. The Chairman (the office alternates between the UK and France), who would traditionally invite the head of one of the wine establishments he represented, was then British and chose to ask Madame Bollinger. Fourteen hundred men rose to their feet in the Great Room at the Grosvenor House Hotel as she entered, as always on such special occasions beautifully dressed by one of her many friends among the great Paris couturiers. Soon afterwards I had the privilege of being one of the guests at a small luncheon at which she was present and her seriousness about the wines served – not only Champagne – was equalled by her personal charm. She was a very great Champagne lady indeed, with a shrewd sparkle in her bright eyes, a gentle voice – but definitely a firm chin.

In the New World, rather surprisingly, there seem to be fewer women who have emerged as personalities of wine in their own right.

South of Santiago in Chile, in the Macul area, Mateus Cousiño, whose first wife had died at an early age, married, as his second, a widow, Maria Gallo; she seems to have been a remarkable woman, interesting herself particularly in the vineyards, which, in this region, have been under vines since 1554. Her influence on the subsequent history and considerable achievements of the firm of Cousiño Macul is still spoken of with great respect.

The Beaulieu Estate in Sonoma County, California, was named by Fernande de Latour, wife of Frenchman Georges de Latour; their daughter married the Marquis Gaston des Pins, a wine grower originally from Gascony, and the Marquise took more than a superficial interest in the running of the wine business, eventually succeeding her mother as President of Beaulieu. Her daughter, Dagmar Sullivan, reserved what was Georges de Latour's original Cabernet vineyard when four of the five main vineyards on the Beaulieu Estate were sold to the mighty firm of Heublein.

In the Napa Valley the outstandingly fine sparkling wine, Schramsberg, (which no European, for legal reasons as well as wine ones, can call 'Champagne') was established by Jacob and Annie Schram, who arrived from the Rhineland in 1842. Annie Schram supervised the planting of the vines, while her husband, a barber, tramped round the farms plying his scissors and razor to make sure that at least some money was coming in. Today's owner of Schramsberg, Jack L. Davies, was fortunate in that his wife, Jamie Louise, took an equally active part in the business. When, in 1966, they were making their first vintage, the crusher broke down, so Mrs Davies took off her shoes and finished the job in the traditional way – with her bare feet!

Daughter of the ebullient Napa personality, Robert Mondavi, Marcia Mondavi is very important and active in the family firm. She has worked in many sections and is now Eastern Vice-President. She conducts seminars and tastings at a high level, including the rather unusual 'component tasting', in which isolated components of various things – sugar, acid, tannin, sulphur – are tasted in water and then in wine. This is a somewhat curious procedure and, although I attended a tasting that Miss Mondavi organised in London, it does not seem to have been repeated since then in Britain.

Madame Lily Bollinger – 'Tante Lily' to many of the Champagne dynasties – making her regular morning rounds in the vineyards on her bicycle.

There are a large number of women, in both the new and old worlds, in charge of wine tours and courses arranged at wineries, but special mention should be made of the chatelaines who preside at many of the great estates. These ladies don't restrict their activities to seeing that guests visiting or staying there are made welcome and comfortable. Details of how certain wines should be fitted into the menus (maybe for several hundred people, sometimes only for a few) and background knowledge, not only of the wines of the house but of the region, are routine for them. At the risk of offending by mentioning only two of the many, the elegant Château de Saran, Moët et Chandon's property outside Épernay and the rose-coloured Château Loudenne, the Gilbey estate in the north of the Médoc, are famous throughout the wine world for their series of 'ladies'.

In the Cape region of South Africa one of the first mountain farms to be settled was that of Muratie – the word comes from the Dutch, meaning 'ruin', because the house is supposed to have been rebuilt after a fire in the early days. The first records show that, by 1685, it was under vines. A subsequent owner, arriving in South-West Africa in 1907, built up the estate's reputation for fine wine and, when he died in 1959, his daughter, Annemarie Canitz, took over management of the farm, which she still runs. But there are many women who, in the 'fairest vineyards' of the Cape, work alongside their husbands very much as must have happened in former times, the ladies only keeping in the background as regards publicity, never when the practical work to do with wine-making is involved.

One 'outsider' who, in very recent times, has made a new contribution to the Cape wine scene, is Mrs Phyllis Hands, of The Cape Wine Academy; this, run from the Oude Libertas Centre at Stellenbosch, now includes several thousand graduates and has influenced the teaching on wine throughout the Republic of South Africa; Cape Wine Academy women students are to be found in many of the great wine organisations and wineries which is a tribute to their accomplishments as well as to their charm and appearance. Their detailed knowledge of all aspects of vines as well as wine is impressive; it would certainly have been intimidating to me had I not felt I was among friends when I visited them and attended some of their sessions. It is almost unfair to reflect that this incomparable wine region should also be peopled by some of the most lovely girls and beautiful women I have ever seen. The girls who conduct the courses at the mighty Koöperative Wijnbouwers Vereniging at Paarl are equally delectable and informed. Anyone still stuck in the 'women can't really know about wine' rut would get a shock in South Africa!

In Australia the influence of women seems to be somewhat played down. One wonders why this should be so when one visits a wine estate that is a small community, virtually comparable to a medieval property, requiring the attention of the owner's lady in considerable detail. Again, many women work alongside their husbands in some of the newer wineries, in addition to those who organise the tours and act as hostesses to the privileged visitor. It tends to be the wine makers most recently arrived from the UK who do not hesitate to give women equal responsibility with themselves – at least this has been my experience in visiting some regions. There are already respected ladies of wine 'down under' however; the Dean of Oenology of the world-famous Roseworthy College, in the Barossa Valley, Dr Bryce Rankine, says that he enjoys teaching women. One of his students is already a prize-winning wine-maker, but as I have not yet met her, I can't report personally; possibly she is keeping the 'low profile' that was obligatory to those, such as myself, who began to study wine seriously in the UK thirty years ago.

Mrs Phyllis Hands, Principal of The Cape Wine Academy and co-author of an award-winning book on South African wines.

The fact that, nowadays, women win big awards in the wine trade examinations and take on all kinds of responsible jobs, including many in journalism, is, understandably, attended by a considerable amount of publicity. Times have changed, of course. I can only say that, when I began to study wine, it would have been considered unseemly by those who taught me to make any publicity out of my own small achievements. This reticence certainly also applied to the first woman Master of Wine, Sarah Morphew, (a particularly beautiful young woman) who passed the examination in 1970. Similar modesty was displayed by the first person outside the wine trade to be allowed to take this tough examination and who passed it at her first attempt in 1984, my younger colleague, Jancis Robinson. Humility, after all, is one of the prerequisites for being in any way adequate in the world of wine.

There are so many women who line up for awards at the annual bestowal of prizes at Vintners' Hall in London, so many who write regularly in the press and assemble the material for books of considerable importance that there should be nothing remarkable about a woman in the wine world today. Indeed, those of us who are concerned with wine and happen to be women emit sighs of irritation when yet one more journalist decides to do a feature on 'Women in Wine'. It's foolish to think that there's anything remarkable about this. When I began to study for the exams of the wine trade, there was only one thing that concerned me – that at the time of the examinations the men wouldn't crowd

into what was then the solitary ladies' lavatory at Vintners' Hall. In doing my cellar work, I was never allowed to show off by trying to move the casks in the cellar. These are rolled along and then, at a junction in the alleyways between the lines of barrels, may be directed to right or left by a quick turn of the wrist on top of the cask, which sends the barrel spinning on its way. I was never permitted to do this – not because I might run the cask over my feet in executing the proverbial 'flick of the wrist' to turn it, but because, as my various teachers told me, I might damage the cask – which was expensive.

Perhaps amongst all the ladies who have influenced wine, the most astonishing is Dona Antonia Adelaide de Ferreira, (1810–1886). She was born at Regua, right in the heart of the port country. As Ben Howkins in *Rich, Rare and Red* (Heinemann 1982) comments, 'her achievements would be remarkable at any time – in the 19th century and what is still predominantly a masculine world, very heroic. And she inaugurated the tradition of fine wine making'. It is all the more remarkable that this lady has never been the subject of a full-length biography, especially as there still appear to be those who, thanks to a cosy private income, are able to indulge their interests and contribute to research without being subject to the obligations of the hack journalist, who has to write to pay the rent.

Shifting a cask of Cognac in Hennessy's cooperage, which task a skilled workman can accomplish with ease.

Dona Antonia married her cousin, one of the richest men in Portugal; he was the first person in Oporto to own a carriage with horses and he had many of the roads of the city paved for their easier passage. His house in town consisted of one whole side of a square. Up in the Douro region, where vines were planted by the hundred thousand, his estates were vast: one vineyard of a single quinta (farm) covered seven hills and thirty valleys. He died when he was still quite young, leaving Antonia with a boy and a girl, after which his widow married her husband's friend and the manager of his estates, Hosea da Silva Torres; he also died after a short time and she did not remarry.

Portraits of this lady show her as having a somewhat heavy countenance and formidable appearance, but there is obvious competence in the expression of the eyes – she would not have suffered fools gladly, but she would have been kind to the deserving. (And she may have become bored with wasting time sitting for her picture.)

The way in which Dona Antonia ran her estates is respectfully recorded by all who knew her – no detail was too small to receive her attention and it is thought that as a result of this dedication to her task, with which was also associated many charitable activities, she never left either Oporto or the Douro region. However, there is a tale, which I was told when a guest in the area, that she did at one time actually go abroad; her daughter, having attracted the attentions of a 'very important personage' in Portugal, was unwilling to agree to becoming his mistress, so Dona Antonia took her daughter away – and it is thought that she came to England. There she remained, until the situation had cooled down, when she was able to return, eventually seeing her daughter married to the man of her choice. No documentation, as far as I know – but what sympathy and courage!

Perhaps the most publicised episode in this lady's life was when, on May 12th, 1862, she was due to lunch at Quinta de Vargellas, the property now owned by Taylor's, as was Joseph James Forrester, the great personality ennobled by the Portuguese as 'Barão'. Brilliant, remarkably erudite as regards all aspects of the Douro, his wonderfully detailed maps are in use to this day. Together with the cook from the Hôtel de Paris in Oporto, Baron Forrester and Dona Antonia, with her ladies in attendance, were returning from the Ferreira estate, Quinta da Vesuvio. Forrester's usual boat was for some reason out of service and the party took a smaller one. In the rapids at the Cachaŏ de Valeira – which to this day, even with the level of the river raised considerably, are terrifying, the black water flowing fast between precipices of granite – the little boat overturned in the current. Forrester, his body probably weighed down by a money belt which he was wearing in order to pay his workers, was never found, but Antonia and the other women floated to safety – they were wearing crinolines, which, holding the air within them, acted as life belts and bore them safely to a sandbank, from which they were later rescued.

(I've not been able to find out what happened to the cook, but perhaps he clung on the skirts or maybe the pantalettes of one of the women.)

There's another surprise in store for those who find it remarkable that there are a number of women in the wine trade today and that outside it, a fair number of women study it seriously. The quantity of taste buds is the same in both sexes – and there is nothing new about women working in the wine trade. In 1865 William Winch Hughes founded a business in Mark Lane in the City of London, calling it, after the Queen, Victoria Wine. Hughes believed that ordinary people should be able to buy good wine, from a number of sources in respectable surroundings, so that there need be no hesitation about entering the shop, or any comment passed on those seen coming out. He not only started something new by making a wine shop a clean, orderly place, with wines on show – not usual at the time – to run each branch he appointed a woman.

There were 87 branches of Victoria Wine by the time of the Diamond Jubilee in 1887 and the manageresses were 'ladies selected with discretion for business capabilities and ladylike manners'; they had to wear black dresses and aprons, being forbidden to sport ribbons or jewellery and were obliged to part their hair in the middle, with a bun at the back. Although deliveries were made by boys wheeling hand barrows, or, in the country, driving pony carts, contemporary drawings show the interior of Victoria Wine shops and cellars, where women assistants are examining bottles and binning them, washing bottles preparatory to filling and generally conducting the routine business of both shop and cellar. Transactions were businesslike – and all purchases had to be paid for on the spot in cash.

It is sad that most of the records of this remarkable venture were destroyed by a

A festive season's selection seems even to have included a packet of the British national beverage, tea.

World War II bomb in 1941. Still, the wines that the manageresses sold were extremely varied and one list that survives from 1896 includes 27 ports, 22 sherries, 7 different Sauternes and various wines that might be thought of as novelties on lists even today – from the Roussillon region of France, from Australia, California, the Canary Islands and even a Welsh whisky.

Aphrodisiacs must be considered as a postscript – but possibly a relevant one. Throughout the centuries, many foods and even more wines have been recommended as incitements to desire. Potions containing gold or silver dust were, as has been mentioned, sup-

HOW SIR TRISTRAM DRANK OF THE LOVE DRINK

posedly preservatives of youthful forces. The combination of oysters and Champagne is, in more recent times, thought to be a stimulant preliminary to amatory exercise. We don't know anything about the exact nature of the 'restorative broths' that are constantly being brought to the heroines of the great pornographic classics when they have given their all in some house of ill fame. Nor do I think that, in the minute phial that Brangäne brings out (instead of poison) to put into the cup drunk by Tristan and Isolde with equally fatal results, there could have been much in the nature of a satisfactory drink. Apart from anything else, there wasn't much for them to swallow! (No opera programme has yet, as far as I know, featured 'Love Potion by kind permission of . . .').

In a delightful light romance, by a lady related to the late W. Somerset Maugham (who really did know something about wine, even though his addiction to the dry martini somewhat disillusions anyone as to the sensitivity of his palate), the heroine, a society woman of the Edwardian period, visits her guardsman lover in his bachelor chambers in St James', where 'they drank Château Yquem and yellow Chartreuse and made love all the afternoon.' Although I cannot speak with the voice of experience, I very much doubt whether they could have done so. They would probably have been sick or in the loo. And I can say, that on the one occasion when I tried the combination of Champagne and yellow Chartreuse, at a party given by a former Grand Duke of Imperial Russia, which took place in a house not a quarter of a mile from my own home, I was obliged to take a taxi back. Even though in those days I could drink a great deal more than I can now, my legs simply wouldn't support me to get there.

It may be, however, that the great rich, sweet wines have practical properties as far as a man is concerned. Men frequenting rather exclusive 'establishments' – who might, therein, feel in need of a restorative – have confided in me that the combination of highish alcoholic strength and sugar has been a useful pick-me-up.

Otherwise, it's reassuring to know that, scientifically, in spite of all the potions and recipes (which at one time actually included crocodile faeces), there is none that will achieve more than the proximity and natural attraction between two people, both of them enjoying the health that usually comes from a good diet and, of course, adequate wine. The relaxing of the inhibitions by alcohol is rather another matter – but this need not be confused with an aphrodisiac. The latter doesn't exist.

left *Illustration by the great artist, Aubrey Beardsley (1872–1898), of the love story of Tristan and Isolde – though the pair seem to be in an exotic garden, instead of on the boat taking them from Ireland to Cornwall.*

P.....and Pong

The mention of women in conjunction with wine nowadays seldom provokes more than the odd masculine, 'Don't you find it rather difficult among all these men?' (Any reasonably feminine woman will certainly share my often expressed view that there's nothing difficult about being surrounded by men – if they are gentlemen. Indeed, an all-female gathering has a depressing effect on me, as if I were back at my loathed boarding school.)

There are the mini-minded women who twitter that of course they leave everything about wine to their husbands . . . and frequently one observes these ladies, who neglect any embellishments of their hair, their faces or their wardrobes. It is not at all surprising to note those same husbands often devoting their attention to women who do know something about wine – and men.

A topic that continues to be introduced is that of scent. 'Don't you have to be ever so careful about not wearing scent to tastings?' Of course – and one doesn't. But, even before the era when men began to wear various toiletries that might be scented, it was apparent that there are smells attached to men as undesirable in the tasting room as a preliminary drench of Chanel Number 5.

Everybody has a personal smell. When well, this is wholesome; when ill, or when the metabolism has been altered because of medication, it can be downright unpleasant. The breath, the sweat and, of course, other excreta can tell a physician a great deal – and any mother knows the difference between the smell of her healthy baby and the smell of the infant who has an upset stomach.

Some notorious womanisers have claimed it was the delicious smell they emanated that made them irresistible – and this years before we knew anything about pheromones and the use of sprays that can lure male animal to female or vice versa, even when natural inclinations may not be particularly powerful. One member of the wine trade told me that a girl friend of his remarked on the smell of raspberries he gave off when they made love . . . I don't know whether, in today's parlance, any particular food or drink smell turns me on – or off. But those whose sense of smell is generally tuned up would find it very difficult to overcome repugnance to a smell, no matter how apparently attractive the other person might seem.

However, there are still ladies who arrive at tastings redolent of 'Joy', 'Je Reviens' or even scents suggestive of the souk. I love scent and a day when I'm going to a tasting and can't wear any is something of a fast day. 'Now I can smoke my pipe,' my teacher used to say when tasting had finished for the day. 'Now I can go and put on something fragrant,' I say when I've finished a session.

What I was once told and have always remembered, as one does trivial bits of information, is that, in the world of scent, the sultry perfumes are bought by ladies who wish they had allure, *mystère*, glamour, 'le sex-appeal' and, alas, haven't, so hope for the best by splashing a sexy smell on themselves. The ladies who, at any age, are not merely full of hope but display the 'lineaments of gratified desire', usually opt for the light, floral fragrances; is this, I have often wondered, because these take them back to the days of their youth and convey to their admirers some nostalgia for the times when 'all the girls were pretty and all the men were strong',

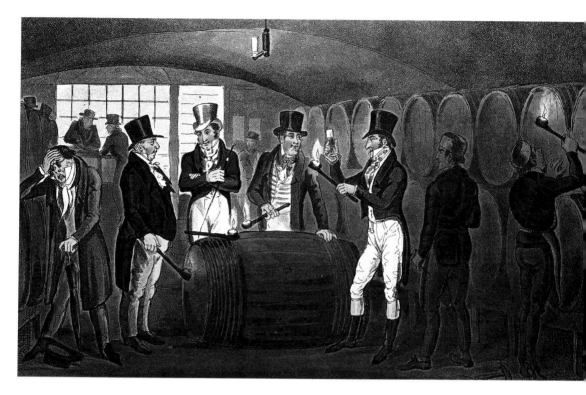

as the trio of antique dames sings in the musical of Ronald Firbank's *Valmouth?*

All I know is that I have about four scents on the go, depending on times and seasons – and that, when I go to a blessedly hot climate, I wear scents that would seem aggressive and vulgar in London, simply because the atmosphere and the circumstance of my sweating (does anyone remember the 'Horses sweat, gentlemen perspire, ladies glow' dictum of pre-1939?) change the way these smells smell to me and, I suppose, to those around me. Certainly, it is necessary to change the scent you use, to avoid becoming so used to it that you have no idea when it may be distracting everyone else. This is what I think happens with some of the otherwise delightful women who emanate their regular perfume even when it is not acceptable

Cruikshank's view of tasting in the London docks, where visitors were given candles stuck on metal batons – these are sometimes still used in very old cellars today, where there is no electricity. One man, on the left, has obviously been drinking rather than tasting – in most excursions into cellars there is usually one person who adopts this unwise mode of deportment.

It's astonishing how quickly a wide space is cleared around the pong porters so that they move about, rather like the Queen at a garden party, where guests are kept at a respectful distance. One sees those just ahead in the tasting line hurrying up, or retreating until the alien bouquet has wafted past. Yet it would be difficult to sniff at incomers at the door and bar the way of same. Indeed, if anybody tried, they might have to block the entrance of men as well, not only because of scented toiletries, but because there are few more acrid smells than those coming from dark suiting, inadequately cleaned with cheap fluid. 'Waiters' armpits', a wine trade friend used to mutter in some restaurants that ought to have known better, and the waves of stale sweat that assail one around many a spittoon can be so unpleasant as to make me resigned to the huge cleaning and laundry bills I pay.

What men do not always realise is that the contents of their pockets can be as aggressively odorous as anything that a woman may put on her face or her hair. Many years ago I was invited to a Bordeaux tasting-room where someone not in the wine trade was already examining some wines. 'Haw, haw! Now we shall not be able to taste anything, shall we – the lady has arrived!'

Beady was the look I directed at that man. I informed him that I could smell what he had put on his (thinning) hair, his after-shave, his boot polish, the fact that his suit had been cleaned with cheap cleaning fluid – and that he had a pipe and tobacco in a jacket pocket. He clapped his hand to this last in considerable surprise.

Recently I was talking with a dear friend at a tasting and remarked that he had some nice Havanas in his breast pocket. 'Can you smell them? Oh dear – I ought to have left them in my despatch case.'

These days, modern dentistry and general hygiene have done away with some of the pongier problems, but there were some friends of the past who deserved all the nasty comments that Shakespeare and his colleagues used to make about foul breath. A particular individual was like the unfortunate schoolmaster in *Clochemerle* (by Gabriel Chevallier) – one contorted oneself so as not to be in the direct waft. 'My mouth may be nasty,' one says if in the slightest doubt. 'You *will* tell me, won't you?' and one breathes hard against one's hand, to try and see if one offends.

It is surprising how often tastings are given in places where other smells have easy entry. There was one office above a sleazy café, where the proprietors clearly fried from morning till night without changing the oil. There was another where the so-called air conditioning merely drew in the cigarette smoke from the firm downstairs. I sniffed with great annoyance at the ventilator grill in the room in a famous club – were we directly above the kitchen where the chef was preparing gallons of mint sauce? No – 'twas the toothpaste of the eminent estate owner, as he circulated, smiling, among those attempting to appraise his fine wines. And often a breeze has borne the aromas of the luncheon menu into many a trade tasting. One is working away, pen poised to note an immediate impression and 'steak and kidney' or 'onions' suddenly seems to surge up from a wine – several times I've actually written the words down before I've realised that, while wines can sometimes smell strange, even bizarre, they do not often smell wholly of food.

My particular dislike is the smell of dirty hair – on man or woman. In any city, hair is virtually impossible to keep really clean if it's trailing on the shoulders.

Yet it isn't always the smells from apparently obvious sources that trail about in tastings.

Years ago I was eyed with great disapproval by a number of men who didn't know me, when I attended a very famous session of a tasting on what was known as 'Ladies Day'. I was myself wrinkling my nose at a definite and pervading smell of some exotic spice (one can cope with garlic on one's breath – chew some parsley or a coffee bean) and, whereas this pong wasn't quite curry, it did have something evocative of the east about it . . . Later, when I commented on this to a member of the wine trade, he said 'Oh yes – Monsieur de . . . (naming the owner of one of the greatest estates), he always reeks of that.' The estate had – and has still – a deserved reputation for outstanding quality wines. Alas, the scented owner (who relinquished his holding soon after I met him, and who does not seem to have

Scientific appraisal by an Italian oenologist – the wine is first being examined for limpidity in a well-designed tasting booth.

been noticed since in wine circles) obviously put his personal perfuming above the glorious bouquet of his estate's wine.

On another occasion, I could not trace the source of a quite violent smell of Johnson's Baby Powder – why would anybody be using this to such an extent that it affected the whole atmosphere? When I was leaning over the spittoon, which was quite a large one, I received such a direct whiff that I looked up – the powder smell came from the beard of a colleague who, I suppose, had been treating it to some form of dry shampooing.

A true smell story that, these days, may amuse more than shock, comes from the household of one of the most historic, dynastic and respected port firms. It may be imagined how

conventional and traditional such families were – indeed, many of them are still delightfully and courteously so. In pre-1939 days most would have been almost 18th century in manners and conduct.

The protagonist had several golden Labradors who were allowed indoors – but not in the dining-room. The patriarch dog, whose name was 'Lion', had reached the age at which it gave vent to really terrible smells from time to time, although, beloved as it was by all, these effluvia merely caused the family and the staff to open windows and doors and flap in fresh air.

During a formal dinner – and the port trade's dinners are, in the most charming way, the apotheosis of formality – the host suddenly exclaimed 'Lion! Lion – get out! You know you're not allowed in the dining-room.' The service of the meal continued – and suddenly, yet again . . . 'Lion – I told you – get out! My dear,' to his wife at the other end of the table, 'get somebody to push him out – it's too disgusting.' 'But, darling,' came the reply, 'Lion hasn't been in the room at all.' . . .

The last glass

In these computerised times, dominated, in many sections of the wine world, by 'panel tastings' in which everything has to be slotted into a table, chart or scale and generally made rather dull, it is arguable as to whether I should conclude this compilation with three pieces of information that I haven't been able to fit in to any other chapter. Here goes anyway.

The first relates to spitting. Oddly, many people are still shy of doing this, although those who are too bashful to do other than drink when faced with twenty or more wines – especially young wines, undrinkable as yet – or a wide selection of rather special ones at a lecture, thoroughly deserve the blurred impression and often uncomfortable gut feelings that result. It isn't difficult to spit wine out and although I do not urge following the instructions I was given years ago – lie in the bath and try to hit your feet – some practice is advisable, if, fully clothed, you are to avoid spitting either on your own feet or those of anyone else.

The record spit stands, as it has done for years, at 11 feet 3 inches and it was set up by a dear friend, John Smithes, of the firm then known as Cockburn Smithes. This establishment trained a number of people to spit in a formidable way, because, in their tasting-room in Gaia, the spittoon was (and possibly still is) a trough under the tasting bench. No spittoon on a stand, box of sawdust in a corner or even a sink received the ejected wine here; it was necessary either to crouch down and put your head under the tasting bench, or stand back and aim from a distance if you were going to get the wine into the spittoon. In fact I have seen some members of the port trade spit over the shoulders of people who were blocking their access to the spittoon – infuriatingly, people *will* gather to chat around it at tastings that include retail customers, who, of course, do have to be considered. It is said that John Smithes once killed a fly with his remarkable trajectory, but he smiles enigmatically when asked about this. The secret, if there may be said to be one, is to take only a little liquid into your mouth and, using the tongue as a type of funnel, push the wine out with as much force as the muscles around the lips can achieve.

Teeth, though, can be a problem. Once at an extremely conventional dinner-party I had my elderly neighbour remove his top plate, to show me how he'd had a small hole made in the plastic, so as to enable him to taste well and I imagine this might have affected his spitting. Some years ago I attended a tasting at which I continually found myself to be overshooting the spittoon – most untidy; it was only after some reflection that I realised that the second of two bridges had been finally fixed in my upper jaw – my spitting, as a result, had far more force than previously and I had to modify my efforts.

There are the many named wines that are, in these days, unidentifiable. One of these is Bastard, mentioned as 'brown and white bastard' in Shakespeare's *Measure for Measure*. (The word 'sack' used to puzzle many, but, thanks to the research of my friend Julian Jeffs, in his masterly book, *Sherry* (Faber), I am sure that it came from *sacar* the verb 'to take out' – in other words, to export, and was used loosely for various wines exported from Spain.)

Bastard seems to have been two different types of wine, but usually sweetish. Before sugar became cheap, of course, sweet wines were prized more than dry. The Bastardo grape is still in use in various parts of the Iberian Peninsula, including the port region and Bastard may therefore have been a wine made wholly from this grape. References to Bastard being a 'compounded wine', however, indicate that it was mixed with something else; this may well have been

honey or some other form of sweetening, making palatable a beverage that, certainly towards the end of twelve months or more in wood (remember, bottles were used as carafes in those days, not for keeping wine) might have been sour. To 'cut' or blend in something else to keep the wine at least vaguely drinkable would be to bastardise it. Wines were – as some of today's purists seldom realise – 'cut' or blended with all sorts of other wines when they might have been improved thereby, and there are lists of comparatively recent date offering some of the greatest Bordeaux reds either *au naturel* or *Hermitagé*, in other words, with a judicious addition of a fuller, fatter, darker wine, of higher alcoholic con-

In the laboratory-like conditions of modern tasting rooms there is plenty of light, benches are usually white – the numbers of the wines can be marked on the surface with a chinagraph – and the spittoon may be just a sink, an adaptation of an industrial handwashing basin, with the flow of water controlled by a bar around the foot, or, as here, a rather elegant copper receptacle.

The Last Drop sketched by Rowlandson, 1829.

tent. There was plenty of wine sent up from the Rioja and Penedès regions of Spain to 'help' various French classics in poor years and there are many growers of Gamay in the Loire who still remember how their wine would travel 'a bit further south', to help out Beaujolais at need, before controls became strict. Hermitage, the deep red wine of the Rhône Valley, was extremely popular and hence gave its name to the process of blending in a wine to make the original more acceptable to a particular market.

My personal theory is that Bastard might have been a term used for oldish wines, coming from no matter where, that had been subjected to some ameliorating treatment so that, even with the new vintage on sale, the old stuff could still be drunk, instead of being made into vinegar or merely tipped away. Brown Bastard might have acquired its tone from being some time in cask and taking on colour from the wood, also from possible skin contact with black grapes, which tint wine via the pigments in the skins. White Bastard might have been kept in a glass vessel instead of wood, or, which I think more likely, could have been blended with some young, shrill white wine that had as yet acquired no colour at all. These days there are ways of putting right anything that may go wrong in wine or, better, of preventing anything going wrong. But in former times one can well imagine the merchant, faced with a cask of sour, thin liquid (perhaps the ship had been held up, or the carrier stopped overlong at some friendly alehouse before making the delivery), despairing of being able to sell the stuff and gratefully receiving the advice of someone who'd worked on a wine estate: 'Add a little honey and about two measures of that really good Malmsey you gave me for lunch – that's right, stir it well. It won't taste like anything else you're stocking, of course – why not give it a completely new name?' Many a chic novelty has been born out of a desperate situation. But we shall never know for sure this side of the Elysian Fields.

An unofficial tradition that, informed gentlemen tell me, is still maintained, is observed at the great cavalry school at Saumur. Here the cadets perform wonderful feats of horsemanship in public. At the military Mass in the Cathedral, trumpets are blown at the Elevation and spurs jangle thrillingly as the officers and cadets kneel. (It isn't all just show, either – the gallantry of the cadets in defending the area in World War II is commemorated by a touching monument nearby – these were, remember, only young teenagers when they fought for France.)

Apparently the cadet who has passed all his examinations, is given a final test. He is provided with three horses, three bottles of Champagne (I haven't been able to discover why Champagne rather than sparkling Saumur, the wine of the locality), three ladies of the town, who are to bear witness later as to his performance, and a night time route of some length and danger across country.

This tale, I am informed by the most elegant and witty of colleagues, Cyril Ray, is also told about a Prussian military academy and, in a somewhat etiolated version in an opera, *The Rising of the Moon*.

One can picture the ordeal taking place in various circumstances, compared with which the rolling of the apprentice cooper in a new barrel is a gentle activity. Given, as Pythagoras or some such person might have said, that the three women are the constants, a test might involve mechanical methods of propulsion, such as three parachute jumps, three hang glide trips over fearsome landscapes, three miles in cars of vintage type (previously sabotaged by fellow candidates, no doubt) three dives into shark-infested waters, or three kilometres on foot, without any weapon, in mamba, rhino and lion reserves.

The candidate has to complete his 'course' within a given time; certainly it might be difficult to tackle in daylight. But the real problem is – in what order does he 'take his fences'? The women, the wine, the Herculean feat? Which aids or harms t'other? The matter has occupied after-dinner conversation for, I believe, generations. It's a pretty problem.

Index

Alicante 97
Aligoté wine 81
Allen, Warner 20, 115
Allesverloren 104
Anghelu Ruju 95–6
Apostelwein 82
Argentina 102
Arsac 98
auction 84–5
Augsburg 86, 88
Australia 102, 141, 154–5
Avery, Ronald 121

Baden-Württemburg 96
balthazar 42
barco rabelo 126
Barossa Valley 143
'Bastard' 170–73
Beaujolais 42, 60, 81
Beaujolais nouveau 72, 77, 79
Beaulieu 102
Beaumes de Venise 95
Beaune 125
beliefs 31–40
Bellarmines 63
Bernkastel 92
Beychevelle 99
bin labels 64–5; see also labels
Blanc Fumé grape 96
Blanquette de Limoux 96
Bollinger, Lily 153
Bon Breton grape 97
Bordeaux 42, 61, 75, 88, 102, 124, 136, 171; see also claret
bottles 23, 42–8, 66, 94–5
brimmer 20
Britain, Great see United Kingdom
Burgundy 42, 45, 74, 81, 88, 121, 123–4

Cabernet Franc 97
Cadillac 99
California 100–101
Calon-Ségur 98
carafes, carafe wines 47, 76
Carbonnieux 148

'carousel' 75–6
Chablis 84
Chambolle-Musigny 92
Champagne 32, 42–3, 68, 79, 81, 95–6, 105–18, 127, 129–30, 147–9, 161; glasses, 55
Chardin, Jean-Baptiste 44
Chartreuse, Yellow 161
Château Ausone 100
Château Beychevelle 99; see also Beychevelle
Château Chalon 130
Château de Saran 154
Château Lafite-Rothschild 97
Château Latour 88, 98
Château Loudenne 154
Château Margaux 88, 91, 98
Château Mouton-Rothschild 89
Château Tahbilk 102
Château Talbot 99
Château Yquem 161
Châteauneuf du Pape 95
Chenin Blanc 97
Chianti 42, 46
Chile 102, 151
Christwein 82
claret 34, 80–81, 85–6, 123, 133
Clicquot, Madame 144, 149–50
Clos Vougeot 121
coaching glass 19
coaster 'wagons' 28
Coates, Clive 98
Cockburn port 121
Cockburn Smithes 29, 170
Cognac 59, 120
Comblanchien 92
'Comet' wines 82
Commandaria 98
coolers 57–8
Coonawarra 102
copita 48, 75
cordials 56
Codorníu 88
corkscrews 68–73, 112
Cos d'Estournel 88

Cossart, Noël 131–2
Cousiño Macul 151
Cousiño, Mateus 151
cups 48, 55
Cyprus 75, 98, 141–2

Davies, Jack L. 152
demijohns 47, 52
Dijon 81
Doktor site 92
Dom Pierre Pérignon 107
Domecq 62
Douro region 157–8
Doxat, John 20
Dreimannerwein 82
drinking horn 21

Échezeaux 84
Egri Bikavér (Bull's Blood) 94
Elefantenwein 82
Elgin glass, the 49–50
'Emperor' chamberpot 49
Entre-Deux-Mers 99
Épernay 117, 154
Épernots (Épernotts) 92
Erbach 92
Evans, Len 102

Ferreira, Antonia Adelaide de 144, 157
fiaschi 46–7
Firenze 84
Fleurie 90, 143
Forbes, Patrick 48
France 77, 79–81, 99

Gallo, Maria 151
Germany 81, 92
Gerumpel 92
Gigondas 95
gin 20, 32, 64, 133
Gironde region 78, 88, 100
glasses, wine 48–56
Goulburn Valley 102
graters 59
Graves district 99, 136
Greece 75
grinders 59

Hambledon 103
Hands, Phyllis 144, 154
Hanoverian glass 133
Harslevelü 96
Harvey's Wine Museum 64
Hattenheim 92
Haut Brion 92
Heiliger Dreikönigswein 82
Held, Anna 115
Hermitage 172
Hochheim 86
Howkins, Ben 157
Hughes, William Winch 158
Hungary 61
Hyams, Edward 140

Italy 80, 86

jeroboam 42
jug 47, 63; *see also*
  'Toby' jug
Jura region 80, 130

Kampen 104
Karchesia goblet 18
Key, Francis Scott 132
Kir, Félix 81
Kneller, Sir Godfrey 52
Kometenwein 82
Kottobos 13, 21
Kues 92
kylix 13

La Mare 103
labels 64–7, 89
Lafite-Rothschild 98
Lágrima 96
Lamarque 99
Lamego 104
Lancret, Nicolas 22
Landshut Castle 92
Latour, Georges de 151
Lazio region 86
Le Montrachet 91
Le Tertre 98
Les Cras 91
Les Groseilles 92
Les Rugiens 91
Les Vaucrains 92
Loire (river) 96–7
London 75, 78
lopo 61, 71
'Loyal Toast' 132, 136–8
Lucia, Salvatore P. 142
Lynch-Bages estate 94

Madeira 46, 75–6, 80, 130–32
magnum 42
Malaga 96–7
Marcobrunn 92
Marsala 76, 80
marsupial 47
martini, dry 32, 161
Mauzac grape 96
Mavrodaphne 94
Mazenot, René 74
Médoc 99, 154
Meerlust 104
methuselah 42
Moët et Chandon 154
Mondavi, Marcia 152
Mondavi, Robert 152
Montefiascone 86, 88
Monteith 58
Montrachet 37
Montrose 88
Morphew, Sarah 155
Morris, Claver 70
Mosel 32, 92, 136
Mouton-Rothschild 98
mugs 63–4
mulling 49
Muscadet 36
Muscat de Beaumes de
  Venise 79
Muscats 79–80

Napa Valley 100, 151–2
nebuchadnezzar 42
New Zealand 102
'Nig' 64
Nuits St Georges 92

octave 75
Oporto 27, 67, 157–8
Orvieto 42, 46
owl cup 48

Palatinate region 75
Palmer, Sir Charles 88, 91
Paris 84, 91
Parker, Robert 40
Pauillac 88
'peg', drinking a 64
Penedès region 172
Penzer, N.M. 64
Pereire family 91
Pineau de la Loire 97
Pinot Meunier grape 96
pipette 59, 61, 71

pisadores 45
Pol Roger 106
Pommard 91
Pomméry 117, 146
porrón 46, 62
port 32, 67, 75, 80, 104,
  112, 121
port tongs 112
Portugal 84, 157–8
Postgate, Raymond 38, 106, 109
preuve, une ('thief') 59
primeur 78; *see also* Beaujolais
  nouveau
punch bowl 59
punch ladle 58–9

Quinto do Noval port 67

Radgonda Ranina 94
Ray, Cyril 100, 173
rehoboam 42
Reutlingen 82
Rheingau 92, 96
Rheinhessen 96
Rheinpfalz region 75
Rhineland, the 63
Riesling 81, 84–5
rince cochon 81
Rioja region 172
römer 50
Rome 73, 86, 88, 141
Rothschild, Baron Philippe de 98
Russell, Leonard 106

sabrage 111
sack 63, 86
salmanazar 42
Sardinia 95
Saumon Chambord 34
Saumur 78, 110
Sauternes 34
Sauvignon 96
Schillerwein 96
Schluck 48
schnapps 34
schooner 50
Schram, Jacob and Annie 152
Schulwein 82
Schwedenwein 82
sekt 89
sherry 48, 62, 75–6, 80
sherry grape harvest 90
'shot' bottle 67
Sichel, Allan 121, 127

Sichel, Walter 82
smells 164–8
Smith, Benjamin 28
Smithes, John 170
solitaire glass 55, 57
Sonnenuhr 92
Sonoma County, California 151
South Africa 103–4, 154
Spain 46, 62, 88, 92, 97
spices 59
spitting 62, 170
St Estèphe 88
St Hubertuswein 82
St Julien estate 99
St Katherinenwein 82
St Nikolauswein 82
Steinberg vineyard 46
Stellenbosch 103–4, 154
Strumpfwein 82
Swan Mazer 12
swizzle sticks 109

Taittinger, Cathérine 55
tankard 63–4
Tantalus 64
tapas 75
tastevins 73–4

tasting 87, 103, 119–27, 165, 171
tasting cups 73–5
tazza 17
'Tent' 97
testing 126, 167
tinta 97
toasting glass 16
toasts 13–6, 19–20
Toby jug 63
toddy lifter 59
tomboladero 75
TORRES 88
toscanello 43
Trotula 142
Tübingen 82
Tunisia 80
Tuscany 63
Twee Jongegezellen 104

Uiterwyk 104
Uitkyk 104
United Kingdom 67, 81, 134, 155

Valdepeñas 92
velenche 59, 61
venencia 62

Veuve du Vernay 70
Victoria Wine Company 158–9
vin, differences between 79–81
vinegar 38–40
vineyard 92–3
vinho verde 34, 84
vintage 90, 93, 101
Vouvray glass 52

Wachenheim 92
wager cup 63
Watney, Bernard M. and Homer D. Babbage 68
Webster, Daniel 132
Weltevrede 104
Wendeglöcklein 82
Wendewein 82
whisky, malt 34
Williams & Humbert 62
wineskins 43–6
Württemberg 82

Yalumba 102

zarf 55
Zeller, Fernando van 67

The Author and Publishers wish to thank the following for their kind permission to reproduce illustrations contained in this book:

Ancient Art & Architecture Collection 13 top, 18 bottom; Anthony Blake Photo Library 35; Bollinger/Mentzendorff & Co Ltd 152–153; The Bridgeman Art Library 17, 23, 44, 51, 53 top left, 53 top right, 53 bottom, 57 right; Brights Wines/Government of Ontario, Canada 103 top; John Brooks/The Arthur Negus Guide to British Glass, Hamlyn 16; The Cape Wine Centre 103 bottom; J. Allan Cash 92, 93 bottom; Christie's Wine Department 46, 66, 67, 68–69, 84–85, 95, 131, 149; Counsel Limited/Colmans of Norwich 71 bottom; Daily Telegraph Colour Library/G. Harrison 125 top & bottom, Peter Titmus 62; Douglas Dickens 93 top, 143 bottom; Patrick Eager 36, 71 top, 102, 116–117 bottom, 125 bottom; Eileen Tweedie Archive 48; Mary Evans Picture Library 89 bottom, 107 top, 122; Ferreira, Oporto 144 bottom; Food & Wine from France 22, 60, 78, 91, 147; The Fotomas Index 87, 108 bottom, 172; The Worshipful Company of Goldsmiths 55: Master, Fellows and Scholars of Corpus Christi College, Cambridge 12, 14th/20th King's Hussars 49, The Worshipful Company of Vintners 58 top & bottom, 63, James Walker Goldsmith & Silversmith plc member of the H. Samuel Group of Companies 59; Harvey's Wine Museum, Bristol 19, 27, 28, 56, 57 left, 65 bottom, 73, 132, 133; Percy Hennell 29; Michael Holford 15, 18 top, 90 top; Denis Hughes-Gilbey 43, 72 top, 171; The Image Bank 167; Brand Inglis/The Arthur Negus Guide to British Silver, Hamlyn 65 top; The Mansell Collection 21, 74, 108 top, 134, 135, 165; Media Relations Limited 116–117 top, 146; Moët et Chandon (London) Ltd 107 bottom, 111, 115; Mouton-Rothschild/David Russell 89 top; The National Portrait Gallery, London 33, 52; Rex Features 47 bottom, 61, 79, 97; The Sherry Institute 45, 54; Barrie Smith 42, 90 bottom, 99, 143 top; Johan Stander/Struik Books, Cape Town 155; Topham Picture Library 94 top, 100–101, 113, 114, 156, 160; The Victoria Wine Company Ltd 159; Vinos de España 47 top; Veuve Clicquot 144 top, ZEFA 72 bottom, 126 top.